About Food Smarts

Food Smarts is an interactive, learner-centered curriculum for nutrition educators bringing programs to low-income audiences throughout the United States. Included Evaluation Tools are based on the FFY2017 USDA Evaluation Framework. We encourage educators to pair Food Smarts with our online recipe website, EatFresh.org.

The curriculum is intentionally flexible to ensure educators retain control over the type of activity used to meet the stated outcomes. For example, a large, outgoing group might benefit more from a decentralized activity where learning is happening in pairs or trios whereas a smaller group might glean more from a facilitated group discussion. Further, the same activity can be used to achieve different outcomes. Successful Food Smarts facilitators focus primarily on participant engagement and confidence building to put healthy behaviors into practice.

Food Smarts has been used extensively in SNAP-Ed (USDA-funded) programs, as well as in a wide variety of settings including housing communities, shelters, medical clinics, family resource centers, and food distribution sites. Lesson plans of various lengths have been used and evaluated over the years, demonstrating the ability of Food Smarts to meet the programming needs of a wide variety of situations. More specifics on curriculum modification can be found on pages 18-20.

Food Smarts evaluations consistently show statistically significant changes in consumption of fruits and vegetables as well as sugary beverages. For more information about evaluation methods and indicators, please contact Leah's Pantry.

This curriculum has grown and developed since 2006, when the first workshop was held at a transitional housing shelter in San Francisco. In 2021, Food Smarts was updated to align with trauma-informed approaches to nutrition education. We expect this will not be the last revision of Food Smarts and we welcome your comments and feedback.

This Instructor Guide supports the Kids Food Smarts Workbook.

About |

Leah's Pantr
committed to a vision all people being nourished, regardless of socioeconomic status. Our programs and products are designed to ensure all people have access to healthy food and feel competent preparing easy, nutritious meals for themselves and their families. We approach our work through the lens of trauma and resilience, and believe that positive, nourishing food experiences can heal individuals, encourage healthy community norms, promote nutritional security, and support the realignment of broken food systems in low-income communities.
> Learn more at leahspantry.org.

Acknowledgements

Since 2006, Leah's Pantry staff have been fortunate to work alongside a host of talented educators, dedicated partners, and, most importantly, enthusiastic participants from a wide variety of cultural foodways, personal histories, and living situations. We want to acknowledge the thousands of people (literally) who have contributed to the impact of this curriculum through their creativity, shared values, dedication, and open-hearted participation. We look forward to many more years of Food Smarts stories.

California's CalFresh Healthy Living, with funding from the United States Department of Agriculture's Supplemental Nutrition Assistance Program—USDA SNAP, helped produce this material. These institutions are equal opportunity providers and employers. For important nutrition information, visit https://calfresh.dss.ca.gov/cfhl.

Some vector art included was provided by Vecteezy.com and freepik.com. Printed by Amazon KDP in the United States of America.

3rd Edition v.20220207

ISBN: 9798411795172

Table Of Contents

Introduction

Commitments for Successful Implementation

An impactful nutrition education program requires well-prepared facilitators and empowering curricula. But it also requires an appreciation of how structures and systems impact programmatic success and participant outcomes. This can be achieved in part by pairing direct education with policy, systems and environmental (PSE) strategies. Collaboration among funders, organizations, facilitators and policy makers is essential to bring this depth to community nutrition initiatives over the long term. In the meantime, by adopting the commitments below, implementers can support alignment with this larger goal of sustainable systemic change.

Food Smarts Implementers Commit to...	by...	in order for participants to....
A Holistic Vision of Physical and Mental Health	providing accurate, evidence-based information around dietary health and cooking skills	trust the information provided is relevant and actionable; develop skills to identify reliable sources and inaccurate or manipulative information.
	clarifying that health and well-being are not dependent solely on diet, food choices, or individual behaviors	recognize and explore a variety of pathways to achieve well-being.
	avoiding orthorexic food frames and language that promote rigid food rules	develop a healthy, flexible, non-disordered relationship to food.
	identifying food and dietary health as a complex and relational aspect of individual and community life; emphasizing that food is more than nutrients and has significance beyond health or weight	recognize alignment between their lived experience and class topics; elevate the meaning of food in their lives.
	acknowledging the impacts of other factors such as sleep and stress on health and nourishment	become aware of what can short-circuit their good intentions to practice healthy eating.
Compassionate Communication and Facilitation	developing self-awareness about their relationship with food and implicit biases they may hold	feel openness to apply the learning to their own life from connections made with the classes, materials, and community rather than feel judged and misunderstood.
	applying facilitation strategies that create interactive and joyful environments; prioritizing high-quality interpersonal connection using non-judgmental and supportive language	have authentic, trustworthy, and positive experiences that allow for meaningful learning and growth.
	modeling mindful interactions, stress de-escalation, and self-reflection	develop mindfulness and self-regulation strategies that will support flourishing dietary and mental health.

Food Smarts Implementers Commit to...	by...	in order for participants to....
Equity, Inclusion, and Empowerment	creating an empowering space of leadership and shared learning	develop awareness of the complex factors that affect their health and identify ways to engage in community efforts to improve nutrition security.
	celebrating diverse cultural foodways; using cooking as a vehicle for cultural humility, joyful experiences, and equity	cultivate and honor the connection between their cultural identity and their dietary health; cultivate curiosity about other cultures and expand their knowledge and enjoyment of food.
	acknowledging social determinants and other community-level factors that complicate individual efforts to maintain wellness	develop awareness of the complex factors that affect their health and identify ways to engage in community efforts to improve nutrition security.
Facilitating Participants' Access to Resources for Nutritional Security	presenting farmer's markets as a place to support local agriculture, leverage community nutrition support, and find a variety of high-quality, affordable foods	connect to fresh, local produce and the people and land that provide it.
	presenting food pantries as a place to access community nutrition support and find high-quality, culturally diverse foods	view food pantries as a resource of good health in addition to emergency food.
	expanding outreach methods and workshop settings to more broadly engage community members at risk of food security	have broader access to Food Smarts classes that are provided at days, times, and settings that meet their needs.

Food Smarts Key Messages

▊ Message #1: Eat a balanced variety of foods throughout the day.

» Make food choices that honor your health and taste buds while making you feel well.

» Instead of thinking about a "diet", think about a way of eating that includes a variety of food groups.

» Think about the aspects of the food you eat in terms of being "nourishing" or "less nourishing" for your mind and spirit instead of "all good" or "all bad."

» Be mindful of how and what you eat to make nourishing food choices as often as you can.

» Cook as frequently as you can with fruits, vegetables, whole grains, and lean proteins-including plant-based sources, and healthy fats.

» Explore and celebrate cuisines from your culture and around the world for delicious and nutritious meals.

▊ Message #2: Fill half your plate with fruits and vegetables.

» Eating a rainbow of colorful fruits and vegetables is the best way to get the variety of nutrients our bodies need.

» The consumption of fruits and veggies is correlated to a healthier heart, immune system, gastrointestinal system, nervous system, and metabolism.

» Eat fruits and vegetables in a variety of forms: raw, cooked, canned, or frozen.

▊ Message #3: Drink water and avoid sugary beverages.

» Drink more water to quench your thirst. Drinking more water instead of sweetened beverages helps regulate our mood, improve brain function and correlates to improved health.

» Read container labels to find out how much added sugar is in a drink.

» The 5 C's of sugary drinks:

   » **Calories:** Sugary drinks are a source of "empty calories" meaning they have a high calorie count with little to zero nutrients.

   » **Content:** Sweetened drinks fill you up leaving little room for healthier foods.

   » **Calcium-loss:** Excess sugar can prevent calcium absorption, which can make your bones weaker.

   » **Caffeine:** Sugary drinks often have caffeine, possibly causing a person to be anxious and contributing to sleeping problems.

   » **Cavities:** Sugary drinks, even those that are diet, can promote tooth decay and damage teeth due to the acid they contain.

» Read the labels to find out how much added sugar is in a drink.

▊ Message #4: Eat whole grains and high fiber foods.

» To increase fiber intake choose whole grains and plant-based foods such as brown rice, oatmeal, and whole-wheat bread or pasta.

» Fiber helps us feel full, regulates our blood sugar levels, and aids with digestion and metabolism.

» A diet high in fiber has been shown to lower the risk of obesity, heart disease, and diabetes.

8

Message #5: Avoid processed foods; choose more whole foods.

» Eat mostly whole unprocessed foods; avoid ultra-processed foods whenever possible, and choose minimally-processed foods wisely.

» While processing allows foods to be stored longer or made more appealing, it also removes many nutrients from the original foods.

» Choose more foods made from ingredients that you can picture in their raw state or growing in nature.

Message #6: Move your body in enjoyable and safe ways.

» Sit less, move more—on your own or with others.

» Use exercise to improve your mood and energy.

» Be physically active in nature.

» Play actively with your kids.

Message #7: Nourish yourself and others with compassion and connection.

» Eat mindfully by respecting your internal cues of hunger and fullness.

» Show yourself the same kindness and care you'd show a friend or someone you love.

» Pay attention to how marketing in your community and media affect how and what you eat.

» Cook and eat with other people.

» Connect with others by cooking and sharing meals with them.

» Use loving and positive feeding practices with children and others.

Message #8: A healthy and nourished body is not solely dependent on exercise, healthy food, and weight.

» Stress, poor mood, and lack of sleep affect how the body functions and make it harder to practice healthy habits.

» Set simple goals and maintain routines around sleep, exercise, and other self-care activities.

» Manage mood and stress with healthy activities that are calming or energizing.

» A good night's sleep can help reduce cravings for less nutritious foods.

» Remember that healthy bodies come in all shapes and sizes.

Make Every Bite Count With the *Dietary Guidelines*

Executive Summary

The foods and beverages that people consume have a profound impact on their health. The scientific connection between food and health has been well documented for many decades, with substantial and increasingly robust evidence showing that a healthy lifestyle—including following a healthy dietary pattern—can help people achieve and maintain good health and reduce the risk of chronic diseases throughout all stages of the lifespan: infancy and toddlerhood, childhood and adolescence, adulthood, pregnancy and lactation, and older adulthood. The core elements of a healthy dietary pattern are remarkably consistent across the lifespan and across health outcomes.

Since the first edition was published in 1980, the *Dietary Guidelines for Americans* have provided science-based advice on what to eat and drink to promote health, reduce risk of chronic disease, and meet nutrient needs. Publication of the *Dietary Guidelines* is required under the 1990 National Nutrition Monitoring and Related Research Act, which states that at least every 5 years, the U.S. Departments of Agriculture (USDA) and of Health and Human Services (HHS) must jointly publish a report containing nutritional and dietary information and guidelines for the general public. The statute (Public Law 101-445, 7 United States Code 5341 et seq.) requires that the *Dietary Guidelines* be based on the preponderance of current scientific and medical knowledge. The 2020-2025 edition of the *Dietary Guidelines* builds from the 2015 edition, with revisions grounded in the *Scientific Report of the 2020 Dietary Guidelines Advisory Committee* and consideration of Federal agency and public comments.

The *Dietary Guidelines* is designed for policymakers and nutrition and health professionals to help all individuals and their families consume a healthy, nutritionally adequate diet. The information in the *Dietary Guidelines* is used to develop, implement, and evaluate Federal food, nutrition, and health policies and programs. It also is the basis for Federal nutrition education materials designed for the public and for the nutrition education components of USDA and HHS nutrition programs. State and local governments, schools, the food industry, other businesses, community groups, and media also use *Dietary Guidelines* information to develop programs, policies, and communication for the general public.

The aim of the *Dietary Guidelines* is to promote health and prevent disease. Because of this public health orientation, the *Dietary Guidelines* is not intended to contain clinical guidelines for treating chronic diseases. Chronic diseases result from a complex mix of genetic, biological, behavioral, socioeconomic, and environmental factors, and people with these conditions have unique health care requirements that require careful oversight by a health professional. The body of scientific evidence on diet and health reviewed to inform the *Dietary Guidelines* is representative of the U.S. population—it includes people who are healthy, people at risk for diet-related chronic conditions and diseases, such as cardiovascular disease, type 2 diabetes, and obesity, and some people who are living with one or more of these diet-related chronic illnesses. At the same time, it is essential that Federal agencies, medical organizations, and health professionals adapt the *Dietary Guidelines* to meet the specific needs of their patients as part of an individual, multifaceted treatment plan for the specific chronic disease.

chronic disease. A fundamental premise of the *2020-2025 Dietary Guidelines* is that just about everyone, no matter their health status, can benefit from shifting food and beverage choices to better support healthy dietary patterns.

The second is its focus on dietary patterns. Researchers and public health experts, including registered dietitians, understand that nutrients and foods are not consumed in isolation. Rather, people consume them in various combinations over time—a dietary pattern—and these foods and beverages act synergistically to affect health. The *Dietary Guidelines for Americans, 2015-2020* puts this understanding into action by focusing its recommendations on consuming a healthy dietary pattern. The *2020-2025 Dietary Guidelines* carries forward this emphasis on the importance of a healthy dietary pattern as a whole—rather than on individual nutrients, foods, or food groups in isolation.

The third is its focus on a lifespan approach. This edition of the *Dietary Guidelines* highlights the importance of encouraging healthy dietary patterns at every life stage from infancy through older adulthood. It provides recommendations for healthy dietary patterns by life stage, identifying needs specific to each life stage and considering healthy dietary pattern characteristics that should be carried forward into the next stage of life. For the first time since the 1985 edition, the *2020-2025 Dietary Guidelines* includes recommendations for healthy dietary patterns for infants and toddlers.

Consistent and Evolving

Although many recommendations have remained relatively consistent over time, the *Dietary Guidelines* also has built upon previous editions and evolved as scientific knowledge has grown. The *Dietary Guidelines for Americans, 2020-2025* reflects this in three important ways:

The first is its recognition that diet-related chronic diseases, such as cardiovascular disease, type 2 diabetes, obesity, and some types of cancer, are very prevalent among Americans and pose a major public health problem. Today, more than half of adults have one or more diet-related chronic diseases. As a result, recent editions of the *Dietary Guidelines* have focused on healthy individuals, as well as those with overweight or obesity and those who are at risk of

The Guidelines

The *2020-2025 Dietary Guidelines* provides four overarching Guidelines that encourage healthy eating patterns at each stage of life and recognize that individuals will need to make shifts in their food and beverage choices to achieve a healthy pattern. The Guidelines also explicitly emphasize that a healthy dietary pattern is not a rigid prescription. Rather, the Guidelines are a customizable framework of core elements within which individuals make tailored and affordable choices that meet their personal, cultural, and traditional preferences. Several examples of healthy dietary patterns that translate and integrate the recommendations in overall healthy ways to eat are provided. The Guidelines are supported by Key Recommendations that provide further guidance on healthy eating across the lifespan.

The Guidelines

Make every bite count with the *Dietary Guidelines for Americans*. Here's how:

1 **Follow a healthy dietary pattern at every life stage.**
At every life stage—infancy, toddlerhood, childhood, adolescence, adulthood, pregnancy, lactation, and older adulthood—it is never too early or too late to eat healthfully.

- **For about the first 6 months of life,** exclusively feed infants human milk. Continue to feed infants human milk through at least the first year of life, and longer if desired. Feed infants iron-fortified infant formula during the first year of life when human milk is unavailable. Provide infants with supplemental vitamin D beginning soon after birth.

- **At about 6 months,** introduce infants to nutrient-dense complementary foods. Introduce infants to potentially allergenic foods along with other complementary foods. Encourage infants and toddlers to consume a variety of foods from all food groups. Include foods rich in iron and zinc, particularly for infants fed human milk.

- **From 12 months through older adulthood,** follow a healthy dietary pattern across the lifespan to meet nutrient needs, help achieve a healthy body weight, and reduce the risk of chronic disease.

2 **Customize and enjoy nutrient-dense food and beverage choices to reflect personal preferences, cultural traditions, and budgetary considerations.**
A healthy dietary pattern can benefit all individuals regardless of age, race, or ethnicity, or current health status. The *Dietary Guidelines* provides a framework intended to be customized to individual needs and preferences, as well as the foodways of the diverse cultures in the United States.

3 **Focus on meeting food group needs with nutrient-dense foods and beverages, and stay within calorie limits.**
An underlying premise of the *Dietary Guidelines* is that nutritional needs should be met primarily from foods and beverages—specifically, nutrient-dense foods and beverages. Nutrient-dense foods provide vitamins, minerals, and other health-promoting components and have no or little added sugars, saturated fat, and sodium. A healthy dietary pattern consists of nutrient-dense forms of foods and beverages across all food groups, in recommended amounts, and within calorie limits.

The core elements that make up a healthy dietary pattern include:

- **Vegetables of all types**—dark green; red and orange; beans, peas, and lentils; starchy; and other vegetables

- **Fruits,** especially whole fruit

- **Grains,** at least half of which are whole grain

- **Dairy,** including fat-free or low-fat milk, yogurt, and cheese, and/or lactose-free versions and fortified soy beverages and yogurt as alternatives

- **Protein foods,** including lean meats, poultry, and eggs; seafood; beans, peas, and lentils; and nuts, seeds, and soy products

- **Oils,** including vegetable oils and oils in food, such as seafood and nuts

4   **Limit foods and beverages higher in added sugars, saturated fat, and sodium, and limit alcoholic beverages.**

At every life stage, meeting food group recommendations—even with nutrient-dense choices—requires most of a person's daily calorie needs and sodium limits. A healthy dietary pattern doesn't have much room for extra added sugars, saturated fat, or sodium—or for alcoholic beverages. A small amount of added sugars, saturated fat, or sodium can be added to nutrient-dense foods and beverages to help meet food group recommendations, but foods and beverages high in these components should be limited. Limits are:

- **Added sugars**—Less than 10 percent of calories per day starting at age 2. Avoid foods and beverages with added sugars for those younger than age 2.

- **Saturated fat**—Less than 10 percent of calories per day starting at age 2.

- **Sodium**—Less than 2,300 milligrams per day—and even less for children younger than age 14.

- **Alcoholic beverages**—Adults of legal drinking age can choose not to drink, or to drink in moderation by limiting intake to 2 drinks or less in a day for men and 1 drink or less in a day for women, when alcohol is consumed. Drinking less is better for health than drinking more. There are some adults who should not drink alcohol, such as women who are pregnant.

Terms to Know

Several terms are used throughout the *Dietary Guidelines* and are essential to understanding the Guidelines and putting them into action. These terms are defined here:

- **Dietary pattern:** It is the combination of foods and beverages that constitutes an individual's complete dietary intake over time. This may be a description of a customary way of eating or a description of a combination of foods recommended for consumption.

- **Nutrient dense:** Nutrient-dense foods and beverages provide vitamins, minerals, and other health-promoting components and have little added sugars, saturated fat, and sodium. Vegetables, fruits, whole grains, seafood, eggs, beans, peas, and lentils, unsalted nuts and seeds, fat-free and low-fat dairy products, and lean meats and poultry—when prepared with no or little added sugars, saturated fat, and sodium—are nutrient-dense foods.

For most individuals, no matter their age or health status, achieving a healthy dietary pattern will require changes in food and beverage choices. Some of these changes can be accomplished by making simple substitutions, while others will require greater effort to accomplish. This edition of the *Dietary Guidelines* presents overall guidance on choosing nutrient-dense foods and beverages in place of less healthy choices and also discusses special nutrition considerations for individuals at each life stage—infants and toddlers, children and adolescents, adults, women who are pregnant or lactating, and older adults.

Although individuals ultimately decide what and how much to consume, their personal relationships; the settings in which they live, learn, work, play, and gather; and other contextual factors—including their ability to consistently access healthy and affordable food—strongly influence their choices. Health professionals, communities, businesses and industries, organizations, government, and other segments of society all have a role to play in supporting individuals and families in making choices that align with the *Dietary Guidelines* and ensuring that all people have access to a healthy and affordable food supply. Resources, including Federal programs that support households, regardless of size and make-up, in choosing a healthy diet and improving access to healthy food, are highlighted throughout this edition of the *Dietary Guidelines for Americans.*

13

Important Contact Info/Social Media

Important Contact Info

» info@leahspantry.org

» (650) 351-7780

Social Media

Leah's Pantry

» Instagram: @leahspantryorg

» Facebook: facebook.com/LeahsPantryOrg

» LinkedIn: linkedin.com/company/leahspantry

» YouTube: youtube.com/c/LeahsPantryorg

EatFresh.org

» Facebook: facebook.com/EatFreshorg

» Instagram: @eatfreshorg

» YouTube: youtube.com/c/EatFreshorg

Preparing for Your
Food Smarts Workshop

Workshop Best Practices: Checklist

A. Planning and Preparation

❑ Use lesson plan for specific audience and for scheduled week
❑ Complete the EatFresh.org Mini Course for Educators before facilitating first workshop
❑ Solicit a co-facilitator or assistant
❑ Review and plan out activities
❑ Read and understand the pre/post questionnaire
❑ Establish consistent and clear communication with site
❑ Try to shop at the markets in the community where workshops are being held

B. Classroom Setup

❑ Ensure that the space is tidy and set up with trash bins, soap, and paper towels before class
❑ Ensure that sufficient seating is set up for expected number of participants
❑ Ensure materials and supplies are available and ready for use
❑ Follow site requirements for how space should be left afterwards (e.g. trash, tables, chairs, extra food)

C. Classroom Management

❑ Have a plan for conflict management and behavioral challenges
❑ Establish classroom expectations and agreements
❑ Use creative approaches to managing group dynamics
❑ Adopt a strength-based approach
❑ Use professional, validating, and respectful communication
❑ Use self-attuning and self-regulation practices

D. Facilitation

❑ Start and end program on time
❑ Introduce topic/objectives and agenda at each class
❑ Provide clear directions and explanations, leaving time for questions and clarification
❑ Present information without a rigid expectation for outcomes
❑ Use a variety of instruction/facilitation strategies
❑ Periodically solicit participant feedback; ask questions to gauge understanding
❑ Provide opportunity for participants to share what they learned, their thoughts, or their feelings
❑ Be responsive and flexible with agenda based upon participants reaction
❑ Use gentle redirection to keep discussion on topic
❑ Acknowledge and address misleading comments (e.g. "I'm glad you brought that up, I have been reading and hearing a lot about gluten-free diets, however you should also know...")
❑ Ask open-ended questions
❑ Be attuned and responsive to each participant's readiness levels, learning style, and literacy levels

E. Cultural Humility

❑ Incorporate discussion, activities, and recipes that reflect an appreciation and understanding of participants' age, cultural background, education, income level, access to resources, and potential health status
❑ Validate differences and the variety of experiences within the group
❑ Model and promote respect for all groups and communities

❑ Support inclusion and participation of all group members regardless of barriers (including, but not limited to linguistic, physical, intellectual differences)

F.   Curriculum Fidelity

❑ Accurately represent Food Smarts Key Messages and nutrition principles
❑ Avoid promoting specific diets or nutrient specific content
❑ Accurately explain nutrition concepts while adapting to various audiences
❑ Use approved lesson plan for specific audience and for scheduled week
❑ Use EatFresh.org or approved recipes
❑ Promote EatFresh.org Resources (when applicable)
   ❑ EatFresh.org
   ❑ EatFresh.org Mini Course
❑ Use verifiable resources and content such as EatFresh.org and MyPlate.gov

G.   Cooking

❑ Use EatFresh.org or approved recipes
❑ Integrate topic and outcomes for the day into cooking or demo portion
❑ Demonstrate relevant cooking skills
❑ Maintain safe environment for food prep according to the state food handlers standards
❑ Model and explain key hygiene and safety principles

Using and Modifying the Food Smarts Curriculum

Leah's Pantry Food Smarts curriculum was initially designed as a six-week workshop series with pre-test and post-test questionnaires to be administered at the first and last sessions. Other iterations of this curriculum have also been evaluated, including five-week and shorter time frame lesson plans. Recipes and other supplemental material that are approved for use in Food Smarts workshops can be found on EatFresh.org.

In some cases, it can be important to modify lesson plans to fit the group you are working with. However, maintaining consistency with nutrition messages is equally important.

Please note that implementing Food Smarts curriculum consistently as written over time will likely produce outcomes similar to those found in the original evaluation. The Food Smarts evaluation results came from partners who adhered to the lesson plans of the workshop series. Deviation from the lesson plans may result in different outcomes.

We encourage our partners to choose the lesson plan that fits best with their agency and funding requirements.

■ For SNAP-Ed Funded Programs

A Food Smarts workshop series must be completed in its entirety to maintain fidelity to the curriculum. All participants do not have to attend every session during the series, however, the lesson plans must be followed as written for consecutive sessions. SNAP-Ed funded organizations may not choose single activities to teach in a workshop or class setting outside of a full workshop series.

In the case where a modification is desired under SNAP-Ed, Leah's Pantry recommends the following (adapted from California SNAP-Ed Curriculum Modification Guidance Table):

Type of Modification	Guidance for Modification	Examples	Evaluation Requirements
Using Leah's Pantry handouts/ materials outside of a continuous class series.	Print handouts directly from workbooks with the footer text included to give credit to Leah's Pantry.	Using handouts or activities in a one-time or as an add-on to other program.	Not appropriate to evaluate with Food Smarts evaluation tools.
Enhancing lessons with visuals or adding props.	Do not substitute for a core component of the curriculum. Only use materials found on snaped.fns.usda.gov, MyPlate.gov, or other science-based resources.	Using handouts found on MyPlate. gov or encouraging participants to use the USDA SuperTracker to track food intake/ quality and exercise.	This modification should not affect evaluation. Food Smarts tools appropriate.

Using and Modifying the Food Smarts Curriculum (CONTINUED)

Type of Modification	Guidance for Modification	Examples	Evaluation Requirements
Using a recipe for a food demo that is not on EatFresh.org.	Consider the cost, healthfulness, and ease of preparation in addition to concerns of cultural relevancy. Avoid exotic ingredients, claims of medical nutrition therapy, or recipes that require specialized equipment to prepare.	A specific request from workshop participants for a recipe that does not exist on EatFresh.org. Teaching a workshop series to a specific cultural group whose cuisine is not represented on EatFresh.org.	This modification should not affect evaluation. Food Smarts tools appropriate.
Making minor adaptations for cultural or age appropriateness.	Consult with experts, such as cultural representatives. Dietary modifications must meet Dietary Guidelines for Americans.	Adjusting names, stories, recipes, food examples and images, and food demos. Modifying handouts to enlarge font size for older adults.	This modification should not affect evaluation. Food Smarts tools appropriate.
Adjusting schedule of classes to fit needs of participants or site.	Class sessions may be divided over multiple sessions, or multiple classes combined into a single session as long as overall curriculum sequence is maintained and content is not omitted.	Dividing a 90-minute session into two 45-minute classes to fit site schedule. Combining two 90-minute sessions into a 1.5-hour session to improve participant retention.	This modification should not affect evaluation. Food Smarts tools appropriate.
Making major modifications or adapting curriculum for different age, grade level, lifecycle stage, language translation, and/or making significant adaptations for cultural appropriateness.	Modifications should be appropriate to meet learning objectives, activities/content should remain in the order specified in the lesson plan, and core components of the curriculum should remain intact.	Administering the adult English curriculum in another language.	Formative evaluation is likely to be necessary.

Using and Modifying the Food Smarts Curriculum (CONTINUED)

Type of Modification	Guidance for Modification	Examples	Evaluation Requirements
Developing a language translation of Food Smarts materials.	Contact Leah's Pantry staff to get approval. Translated text must be verified and then formatted to match Leah's Pantry style guide.	Translating Food Smarts curriculum into a language that meets community needs.	Conduct formative testing of new materials with intended audience prior to use.
Deleting content and/or activities that are essential to achieving a learning objective.	Not allowed.	Omitting an activity that is a core component of a lesson.	N/A
Inserting additional lessons into a curriculum that are not from reliable sources or contradict the Dietary Guidelines for Americans.	Not allowed.	Using handouts from sources that are not USDA-approved, like individual nutrition/diet blogs or companies marketing dietary supplements or products.	N/A

Food Smarts Workshop Planning Sheet

Site Name:

Address, Room Number:

Workshop Language:

Workshop Day of the Week and Time:

Number of Weeks:

Start Date:

End Date:

Briefly describe the audience:

What types of activities would this population enjoy? (group, small group, individual, etc.)

How will you help this group stay engaged and on-track?

Food Smarts Workshop Planning Sheet (CONTINUED)

What are some concerns you have about leading an effective workshop with this group?

Describe kitchen, if applicable:

Supplies available for use:

Storage area (Large enough for workshop supplies? Secure?):

Tables and chairs (number, shape):

Incorporating Recipes into Your Workshop

Recipes are the way we demonstrate simple cooking skills, show examples of the foods we discuss during class, and reinforce nutrition outcomes. Additionally, a well designed cooking portion increases enjoyment of the class, provides opportunity for participants to form relationships, and encourages repeat participation.

But successfully incorporating recipes can be challenging, especially for facilitators on their own or with a large group. The site setup, access to a kitchen, and time of day are also complications. This section is designed to provide guidance and ideas for several aspects of recipe incorporation.

■ Selecting and Modifying Recipes

These recipes have been taste-tested, contain inexpensive ingredients, and meet nutrition criteria for health.

» **EatFresh.org:** This website is managed by Leah's Pantry and partially funded by California's SNAP-Ed Program, CalFresh Healthy Living. It includes easy to prepare recipes and all information is available in English and Spanish.

» **Leah's Pantry Recipe Book:** These recipes are designed to be made during workshops. They include short and flexible ingredient lists and most are easily made with children of various ages. Our facilitators often modify these recipes depending on produce they have on hand from the Food Bank or farmers market, cultural background of the participants, or participant requests. This recipe book also includes cooking with a rice cooker, microwave, and guidelines for a safe kitchen.

» **SNAP-Ed Connection:** https://snaped.fns.usda.gov/nutrition-education/snap-ed-recipes

■ Characteristics of a Successful Recipe

» **Easy to prepare.** No complicated steps or techniques. No fancy utensils or equipment required.

» **Manageable in the time allowed.** Recipes are given 30 minutes per 90-minute workshop. Generally recipes are prepared at the end—soups and baked goods are exceptions. Prepping in advance (see more on this below) is a good idea, but the total prep required for the home cook should not be onerous.

» **Uses seasonal or Food Bank produce.** Selecting seasonal produce will make it easier for participants to find the ingredients in local markets and less expensive to incorporate into their diet immediately. Foods available through Food Bank pantries are essential during workshops where participants rely on weekly food pantries for food.

» **Able to be modified for preferences, allergies and sensitivities.** Many participants have dietary preferences or restrictions such as gluten-free, nut or dairy-free allergies, or meatless. Learn your participants' allergies and dietary restrictions. Use recipes that are easy to modify (i.e. leaving out cheese, using sugar substitute, etc.) or choose 'low-risk' allergy recipes that don't include common allergens (nuts, wheat, milk).

» **Substitution-friendly.** Stress the importance of resourcefulness and re-cycling ingredients. Encourage participants to use what they already have and not to become discouraged if a recipe includes expensive or unfamiliar ingredients. Substitute! Even when making a recipe "as written," engage participants in a discussion of how substitutions could be used at home.

Incorporating Recipes into Your Workshop (CONTINUED)

◾ Preparing a Recipe with the Group

Suggestions for Basic Cooking Kit

ITEM	NOTES
Vegetable peeler(s)	Get sturdy ones, like OXO Brand
Mixing Bowls	
Box Grater	Great for grating garlic, ginger, cheese, veggies
6-8" Chef's knives	IKEA, OXO, Mundial, Victorinox
Cutting Boards	Lightweight boards
Whisk	
Serving/Stirring Spoon	
Spatula/Turner	
Silicone Scraper	
Can Opener	
Liquid Measuring Cup	
Set of Dry Measuring Cup	
Measuring Spoons	
Salad Spinner	
Scissors	Safe cutting option for kids; hand wash and dry well after use
Sturdy Plastic Disposable Knives	Safe cutting option for younger kids classes
Wavy Cutters	Crinkle Cutter available online or a restaurant supply store. Safe option for kids class.
Small Knives	OXO Mini Santoku, paring knives
Electric Skillet or Large Rice Cooker	Good option if you have no stove access
Hand Crank Blender	Fun for kids classes, REI.com
Electric Blender	
12-14" Sauté Pan/Skillet	
Large strainer or colander	
6 Quart Pot with Lid	
Paper Towels	
Ziploc Bags	
Paper Cups	
Plastic Forks and Spoons	
Disinfecting Wipes or Cleaning Spray	
Paper Food "Boats" or small paper plates and bowls	Find at Costco, Smart and Final, or a restaurant supply store
First Aid Kit	
Dish Soap and Sponge	
Dish Towels	
Storage Bin (with lock, if necessary)	

▇ Engaging participants in recipe assembly/preparation:

» Ask them what they'd add at home: what would appeal to their family, any 'ethnic' spices they would add, ingredients from their gardens, etc.

» Don't confuse shyness with lack of interest. Sometimes a group might be reticent to jump up and help when asked "Do you want to help?" Sometimes handing them a knife and saying "Please chop this carrot while I show how we'll create the dressing," can bring a person out of their shell.

» Ask them why a certain dish is healthy; gauge their absorption of material you have covered throughout the course of the session.

» Ask whether they are familiar with these ingredients, and where they get them from.

» Enlist their help in determining which recipes to make. Many times participants have great ideas, or you will have an opportunity to make a healthier version of a favorite meal.

» Make sure you know a little bit about client kitchens so that you don't make assumptions about utensils or equipment they have.

▇ Incorporating Food Smarts outcomes into recipe preparation:

» Review nutrition labels on ingredients used in workshops (this is sometimes difficult when using food provided by the Food Bank or bulk food that has no label).

» Consider how to make fast food healthier, add veggies whenever possible.

» Ask participants if they incorporated their SMART goals, lessons, and recipes into their diet that week.

▇ Tips for a successful food demo (one where participants are just watching):

» You may read the entire recipe aloud with your whole group before beginning to touch on key points.

» Have clients narrate what you are doing, why you chose those ingredients, and what outcomes you are highlighting and utilizing from lessons past.

» Set up the room to make sure everyone has a good view. Consider setting up chairs in an arc, or having clients stand around the table.

» The simpler the better. You need to be able to talk, field questions, and cook simultaneously.

» Prepare as much as possible in advance so there aren't lulls of just one activity that participants are likely to already know how to do (peeling large amounts of garlic, etc.)—unless you have a lot of spoken material to cover and can multi-task. A good idea is to prepare 80% of the veggies that need chopping. This way, you can still demonstrate knife skills and ways to prepare each veggie, but the heavy lifting is out of the way—allowing you to focus more on technique.

» Don't try to talk over the blender.

» Use the Food Demonstration Planning Template on page 29 to plan your demonstration in advance.

» Share where you got the ingredients from. Avoid shopping at tiny grocery stores or markets. Try to shop at the markets closest to the participants.

Other Preparation Considerations:

» If possible coordinate with the Food Bank to see what participants will be receiving/have received that week so you can incorporate the same (or similar yet healthier!) items.

» Line up ingredients in order with corresponding measurement tools.

» Know ingredient names in a few languages.

» Check for mold and other trouble signs before using ingredients in a recipe (yogurt parfait recipe would be moot if the yogurt from last week's class went bad!).

» Preheat the oven when you walk in the door if doing a baked item.

Cooking with Kids at Different Ages

Kids love hands-on cooking, but you may need to modify lessons depending on grade level and group size. Always make sure kids wash hands well before beginning and wear gloves (or sit out) if recently sick or cut.

█ Grades K-2

Kids at this age do best taking turns or making items individually. They are tempted to taste ingredients—when appropriate, have kids do this formally beforehand. Then during recipe prep, remind them often not to put ingredients in their mouths or touch their faces. If the group is large, choose recipes where kids assemble their own portions (i.e. yogurt parfaits or sandwiches, etc.).

Kids this age can:

- » crack eggs
- » crumble ingredients like cheese
- » cut soft items (with scissors or plastic knives)
- » juice citrus fruits
- » knead dough
- » mash soft fruits and vegetables
- » measure, with help
- » pick off stems and leaves
- » set up (arrange items on a platter, for example)
- » roll/wrap foods, such as wrap sandwiches
- » scoop
- » spin
- » spread butter cream cheese, or dip
- » stir/mix/whisk... always a favorite
- » tear leaves, etc.
- » use an apple peeler
- » use a food mill
- » use a mortar and pestle
- » wash fruits and vegetables
- » help clean up! (avoid chemical cleaners by using a spray bottle with water and a bit of vinegar)

█ Grades 3-6

Kids this age can work more cooperatively. Consider recipes that allow you to assign specific tasks to different groups. Kids are more open to technique demonstration at this age and especially enjoy knife demonstrations. They can also begin to practice "adult" techniques such as knife skills with plenty of supervision.

In addition to easier tasks, kids at this age can also:

- » blend items by hand or in a blender
- » chop and slice with real knives, given close supervision; you may also use cut-safe gloves or kid knives
- » collect compost
- » double or triple recipes
- » grate
- » read recipes
- » saute, scramble, and flip stovetop items with close supervision
- » season food
- » preheat an oven, check baked items for doneness

█ Grades 7-12

Kids at this age can complete most tasks described in a recipe, given appropriate supervision. Cooking with this age group also provides excellent opportunities to teach or reinforce learning of math skills, such as adding or multiplying fractions or graphing food waste over time. They can also start to improvise or use their own ideas to improve upon recipes, and benefit from learning simple recipes they can prepare at home with common ingredients—scrambled eggs, salad dressing, veggie quesadillas, or basic pasta sauce.

Content adapted from LifeLab.org.

5 Classroom Management Tips for Working with Kids

1. *Use your everyday indoor voice.* Kids will adapt to your tone; if you speak very loudly, kids will too. You'll also lose your voice!

2. *Don't begin until the group is quiet and paying attention.* You may remind them that the longer it takes to settle and focus, the less time they have for their recipe.

3. *Use hand signals and other non-verbal cues.* For example, choose a specific "quiet down" reminder to use when the room gets chaotic: clap three times, raise your hand and have kids do the same, switch off the lights, etc.

4. *Have a plan for addressing behavior issues.* Challenges are less likely to occur when kids are busy. Nevertheless, coordinate with other site staff in advance about how to deal with behavior issues as they occur, especially in schools. Then explain your expectations and safety rules to kids clearly at the beginning of each activity. In particular, kids who are acting unsafe—for example running around or grabbing/waving knives—must be immediately removed from an activity. (You may wish to have a worksheet or other independent task available for these kids to do. Sometimes though, all that's necessary is to give a child who is "acting up" a unique job that feels important to them.)

5. *Get help if you need it!* Classroom management can be tough with large groups, or in spaces that aren't set up for cooking. Plan ahead to have staff or volunteer support in these situations, especially with younger children.

Food Demonstration Planning Template

Recipe Title: _____

EQUIPMENT/MATERIALS	INGREDIENTS

Recipe Modifications to Suggest:

Handout:

Healthy Nutrition Message to Highlight:

Culinary Skill to Demonstrate:

Food Bank-Friendly Items to Show:

Ingredients to Prep Ahead of Time (if any):

Food Smarts Workshop

Site Name _____

First Name: _____

1. **Can you cook/prepare food?**

___ 😞 I <u>cannot</u> do this.

___ 😐 I am <u>not sure</u> I can do this.

___ 🙂 I can do this <u>with help</u>.

___ 😃 I can do this <u>on my own</u>.

2. **Can you read and follow a recipe?**

___ 😞 I <u>cannot</u> do this.

___ 😐 I am <u>not sure</u> I can do this.

___ 🙂 I can do this <u>with help</u>.

___ 😃 I can do this <u>on my own</u>.

3. **Can you measure ingredients when making a meal?**

___ 😞 I <u>cannot</u> do this.

___ 😐 I am <u>not sure</u> I can do this.

___ 🙂 I can do this <u>with help</u>.

___ 😃 I can do this <u>on my own</u>.

4. What do you think about the fruits and vegetables below?

Fruits & Vegetables		I like this a lot. 😀	I like this a little. 🙂	I do not like this. 🙁	I don't know what this is. ❓
Apples					
Broccoli					
Cabbage					
Carrots					
Cauliflower					
Cooked Greens					
Corn					
Clementines (Cuties)					
Cucumbers					
Grapes					
Green Beans					
Lettuce/Salad					
Melons					
Oranges					
Peas					
Pears					
Sweet Potatoes					
Tomatoes					

5. Are there other <u>fruits</u> that you really like?

___ Yes   ___ No

If yes, what kind? _____

6. Are there other <u>vegetables</u> that you really like?

___ Yes   ___ No

If yes, what kind? _____

7. Choose the sentence that best matches what you think about <u>eating vegetables</u>:

___ I don't think about eating vegetables, and I don't eat vegetables.

___ I think about eating vegetables because my parent or guardian wants me to eat them, but I don't eat them.

___ I am deciding which vegetables I want to eat and plan to start eating them soon.

___ I try to eat at least 1 type of vegetable every day.

___ I eat more than 1 type of vegetable every day.

8. Choose the sentence that best matches what you think about <u>drinking sugary drinks</u>, such as sports drinks, energy drinks, juice, or sodas (not diet).

___ I want to drink more sugary drinks than I am now.

___ I want to drink the same amount of sugary drinks as I always have.

___ I am thinking about drinking fewer sugary drinks than I am now.

___ I drink fewer sugary drinks than I used to.

9. Yesterday, did you eat any vegetables? Vegetables are all cooked and uncooked vegetables; salads; and boiled, baked, and mashed potatoes. ***Do not count*** french fries or chips.

___ No, I didn't eat any vegetables yesterday.

___ Yes, I ate vegetables 1 time yesterday.

___ Yes, I ate vegetables 2 times yesterday.

___ Yes, I ate vegetables 3 or more times yesterday.

10. Yesterday, did you eat fruit? Include fresh, frozen, or canned. *Do not count* fruit juice.

___ No, I didn't eat any fruit yesterday.

___ Yes, I ate fruit 1 time yesterday.

___ Yes, I ate fruit 2 times yesterday.

___ Yes, I ate fruit 3 or more times yesterday.

11. Yesterday, did you drink any water, such as from a glass, bottle, or a water fountain?

___ No, I didn't drink any water yesterday.

___ Yes, I drank water 1 time yesterday.

___ Yes, I drank water 2 times yesterday.

___ Yes, I drank water 3 or more times yesterday.

12. Yesterday, did you eat any corn tortillas or bread, tortillas, buns, bagels, or rolls that were brown (not white)?

___ No, I didn't eat any of these foods yesterday.

___ Yes, I ate one of these foods 1 time yesterday.

___ Yes, I ate one of these foods 2 times yesterday.

___ Yes, I ate one of these foods 3 or more times yesterday.

13. Yesterday, did you drink any sport drinks, energy drinks, or fruit-flavored drinks? *Do not count* 100% fruit juice or diet drinks.

___ No, I didn't drink any of these drinks yesterday.

___ Yes, I drank one of these drinks 1 time yesterday.

___ Yes, I drank one of these drinks 2 times yesterday.

___ Yes, I drank one of these drinks 3 or more times yesterday.

14. Yesterday, did you drink any regular (not diet) sodas or soft drinks?

___ No, I didn't drink any regular (not diet) sodas or soft drinks yesterday.

___ Yes, I drank regular (not diet) sodas or soft drinks 1 time yesterday.

___ Yes, I drank regular (not diet) sodas or soft drinks 2 times yesterday.

___ Yes, I drank regular (not diet) sodas or soft drinks 3 or more times yesterday.

Food Smarts Workshop

Site Name _____

First Name: _____

1. Can you cook/prepare food?

___ 😞 I <u>cannot</u> do this.

___ 😐 I am <u>not sure</u> I can do this.

___ 🙂 I can do this <u>with help</u>.

___ 😃 I can do this <u>on my own</u>.

2. Can you read and follow a recipe?

___ 😞 I <u>cannot</u> do this.

___ 😐 I am <u>not sure</u> I can do this.

___ 🙂 I can do this <u>with help</u>.

___ 😃 I can do this <u>on my own</u>.

3. Can you measure ingredients when making a meal?

___ 😞 I <u>cannot</u> do this.

___ 😐 I am <u>not sure</u> I can do this.

___ 🙂 I can do this <u>with help</u>.

___ 😃 I can do this <u>on my own</u>.

4. What do you think about the fruits and vegetables below?

Fruits & Vegetables		I like this **a lot**. 😃	I like this **a little**. 🙂	**I do not like this**. ☹️	**I don't know** what this is. ❓	I tried this for the **very first time** during the Food Smarts classes.
Apples						
Broccoli						
Cabbage						
Carrots						
Cauliflower						
Cooked Greens						
Corn						
Clementines (Cuties)						
Cucumbers						
Grapes						
Green Beans						
Lettuce/Salad						
Melons						
Oranges						
Peas						
Pears						
Sweet Potatoes						
Tomatoes						

5. Are there other <u>fruits</u> that you really like?

___ Yes   ___ No

If yes, what kind? _____

6. Are there other <u>vegetables</u> that you really like?

___ Yes   ___ No

If yes, what kind? _____

7. Choose the sentence that best matches what you think about <u>eating vegetables:</u>

___ I don't think about eating vegetables, and I don't eat vegetables.

___ I think about eating vegetables because my parent or guardian wants me to eat them, but I don't eat them.

___ I am deciding which vegetables I want to eat and plan to start eating them soon.

___ I try to eat at least 1 type of vegetable every day.

___ I eat more than 1 type of vegetable every day.

8. Choose the sentence that best matches what you think about <u>drinking sugary drinks</u>, such as sports drinks, energy drinks, juice, and sodas (not diet).

___ I want to drink more sugary drinks than I am now.

___ I want to drink the same amount of sugary drinks as I always have.

___ I am thinking about drinking fewer sugary drinks than I am now.

___ I drink fewer sugary drinks than I used to.

9. **Yesterday, did you eat any vegetables?** Vegetables are all cooked and uncooked vegetables; salads; and boiled, baked, and mashed potatoes. ***Do not count*** french fries or chips.

___ No, I didn't eat any vegetables yesterday.

___ Yes, I ate vegetables 1 time yesterday.

___ Yes, I ate vegetables 2 times yesterday.

___ Yes, I ate vegetables 3 or more times yesterday.

10. **Yesterday, did you eat fruit?** Include fresh, frozen, or canned. *Do not count* fruit juice.

___ No, I didn't eat any fruit yesterday.

___ Yes, I ate fruit 1 time yesterday.

___ Yes, I ate fruit 2 times yesterday.

___ Yes, I ate fruit 3 or more times yesterday.

11. **Yesterday, did you drink any water, such as from a glass, bottle, or a water fountain?**

___ No, I didn't drink any water yesterday.

___ Yes, I drank water 1 time yesterday.

___ Yes, I drank water 2 times yesterday.

___ Yes, I drank water 3 or more times yesterday.

12. **Yesterday, did you eat any corn tortillas or bread, tortillas, buns, bagels, or rolls that were brown (not white)?**

___ No, I didn't eat any of these foods yesterday.

___ Yes, I ate one of these foods 1 time yesterday.

___ Yes, I ate one of these foods 2 times yesterday.

___ Yes, I ate one of these foods 3 or more times yesterday.

13. **Yesterday, did you drink any sport drinks, energy drinks, or fruit-flavored drinks?** *Do not count* 100% fruit juice or diet drinks.

___ No, I didn't drink any of these drinks yesterday.

___ Yes, I drank one of these drinks 1 time yesterday.

___ Yes, I drank one of these drinks 2 times yesterday.

___ Yes, I drank one of these drinks 3 or more times yesterday.

14. **Yesterday, did you drink any regular (not diet) sodas or soft drinks?**

___ No, I didn't drink any regular (not diet) sodas or soft drinks yesterday.

___ Yes, I drank regular (not diet) sodas or soft drinks 1 time yesterday.

___ Yes, I drank regular (not diet) sodas or soft drinks 2 times yesterday.

___ Yes, I drank regular (not diet) sodas or soft drinks 3 or more times yesterday.

16. Tell us what you think.

	A lot 😄	A little 🙂	I did not like 🙁	I am not sure ❓
I liked the instructor.				
I liked how the instructor let me participate in the class.				

	Yes 😄	Maybe 🙂	No 🙁	I am not sure ❓
I would tell my friends to take this class.				

Lesson Plans

How to Use the Lesson Plans

» Lengths of lesson/activity are rough estimations. Actual time varies depending on group size and format.

» Recipe preparation time is a suggestion and depends on preparation format and type of recipe.

» With recipes that require simmering or baking, group may want to begin recipe preparation prior to or between lessons/activities so the dish may have time to cook.

Key

 EatFresh.org Mini Course plan

 Six-week plan

 Five-week plan

 90-minute plan

 60-minute plan

IG   Indicates Instructor Guide only

*   Indicates Workbook handout only

Setting the Stage for Healthy Habits // WEEK 1

Lesson Objective:
To consider personal ideas about food and health and look forward to a healthy life.

Time	Topics	Workbook Reference
15 min.	**Getting Started** Welcome and Introductions Pre-Workshop Survey (when applicable); Attendance	
10 min.	**Taste Test**	p. 7
5 min	**Opening Question** *Why do you want to nourish and take care of your body? Besides eating nourishing food, what are other ways you can take care of your body?*	
15 min.	**Food Collage** » Make a collage about health and nutritious food.	p. 8
15 min.	**Your Healthy Life/Your Healthy Goals** » Map out a healthy vision for the future then identify smaller steps that support the vision. Track progress each week.	p. 9-11
10 min.	**Kitchen Safety** » Participants learn the basics of kitchen safety.	p. 18*
20 min.	**Recipe Demonstration or Activity (see EatFresh.org for ideas)**	

Supplemental Handouts and Activities

» How to Read a Recipe, p. 20

» Cooking with Eatfresh.org, p. 15*

» Measuring, IG p. 92

» Glossary of Recipe Terms, p. 19

Building a Wholesome Diet // WEEK 2

Lesson Objective:
To learn some fundamentals about what types of foods make up a healthy diet.

Time	Topics	Workbook Reference
5 min.	**Welcome and Introduction**	
10 min.	**Taste Test**	p. 7
	SMART Goal Check-in	p. 11
5 min.	**Opening Question**	
	What does good nutrition mean to you or your family?	
15 min.	**What's On MyPlate?**	p. 24-25
	» Read about MyPlate food groups and draw a MyPlate meal.	
15 min.	**My Family's Rainbow/Eat the Rainbow!**	p. 35-36
	» Categorize fruits and vegetables according to color and the nutrients they provide and determine which colors might be missing from the diet.	
15 min.	*Choose one of the following activities:*	
	Food Group Bingo	p. 28
	» Match foods to their corresponding food groups in a game of BINGO.	
	Healthy Hopscotch	IG p. 87
	» Play a game where foods are categorized into one of the 5 food groups	
	Restaurateur	IG p. 98
	» Invent a menu featuring creative uses of whole foods.	
25 min.	**Recipe Demonstration or Activity (see EatFresh.org for ideas)**	

Supplemental Handouts and Activities

» MyPlate/Healthy Eating Plate, p. 26-27

» Garden Sort, p. 42

» Fuel Your Brain, p. 45*

» Setting the Table and Eating Together, p. 22*

» Food Journal (suggest participants complete this activity at home), p. 30

Lesson Objective:
To explore the spectrum of food processing and the advantages of eating whole foods.

Time	Topics	Workbook Reference
5 min.	**Welcome and Introduction**	
10 min.	**Taste Test**	p. 7
	SMART Goal Check-in	p. 11
5 min.	**Opening Question**	
	What are some of the reasons you eat fast or processed food or drink sugary beverages? What do you like about these items?	
20 min.	*Choose from the following:*	
	Seed to Plant to Table	IG p. 101
	» Explore where different foods come from.	
	From Grain to Flour to Bread	IG p. 82
	» A hands-on experience of learning how grains become flour and the differences between whole wheat and white bread.	
	Grain Game, Bean Game	p. 38-41
	» Match grain and bean samples to their name and discuss possible ways of cooking each one.	
15 min.	**Food Processing**	p. 32-33
	» Read about different degrees of food processing and evaluate foods according to how processed they are.	
	Building Your Fire	p. 34
	» Name foods that fuel your body for a long time.	
10 min.	**Make These Meals Healthier**	p. 29
	» Review sample meals and suggest ways of making them healthier.	
25 min.	**Recipe Demonstration or Activity (see EatFresh.org for ideas)**	

Supplemental Handouts and Activities

» The Leah's Pantry DO EAT Food List, p. 12-13*

» Make Half Your Grains Whole, p. 37

» Plant Parts We Eat, p. 43

Understanding Labels and Ingredients // WEEK 4

Lesson Objective:
To learn about and how to use the information found on food packaging.

Time	Topics	Workbook Reference
5 min.	**Welcome and Introduction**	
10 min.	**Taste Test**	p. 7
	SMART Goal Check-in	p. 11
5 min.	**Opening Question**	
	How does the information on a food container or package influence whether you buy or eat it?	
20 min.	**Don't Call Me Sugar!**	p. 48
	» Learn different terms for sugar with a word search.	
	Rethink Your Drink	p. 46-47
	» Guess the amount of sugar in various drinks and learn how to drink more water.	
15 min.	**Nutrition Words to Know**	p. 51
	» Learn about some of the nutrition terms found on a label by matching them with their definitions.	
	Food Labels—Nutrition Facts	p. 52-53
	» Identify and discuss key parts of the Nutrition Facts label.	
10 min.	**Food Label Scavenger Hunt**	p. 54
	» Compare and analyze two Nutrition Facts labels to determine the healthier choice.	
25 min.	**Recipe Demonstration or Activity (see EatFresh.org for ideas)**	
	Closing Question: *Besides eating healthy food, what are other ways to be healthy?*	

Supplemental Handouts and Activities

» Eating Out and Staying Healthy, p. 64

» Spice is Nice, IG p. 103

Smart Shopping and Planning // WEEK 5

Lesson Objective:
To consider how food is marketed and develop skills for shopping and planning healthy meals.

Time	Topics	Workbook Reference
5 min.	**Welcome and Introduction**	
10 min.	**Taste Test**	p. 7
	SMART Goal Check-in	p. 11
5 min.	**Opening Question** *How do you help your family when it's time to buy groceries or plan a meal?*	
15 min.	**Anatomy of a Grocery Store/Outsmarting the Grocery Store** » Participants map out their usual grocery store to indicate where the healthy food is placed, and discuss common supermarket tactics.	p. 56-57
15 min	**Food Marketing** » Identify common tactics employed in food advertising to influence consumers.	p. 59
15 min.	**Creating a Meal Plan & Grocery List** » Practice meal planning and preparing a sample grocery list.	p. 58
25 min.	**Recipe Demonstration or Activity (see EatFresh.org for ideas)**	

Supplemental Handouts and Activities
» Eating In-Season, p. 44*

» Healthy Swaps, p. 50*

» Creating a Recipe, IG p. 70

» Superstar Ingredients, p. 21*

Lesson Objective:
To explore holistic practices for good health.

Time	Topics	Workbook Reference
5 min.	**Welcome and Introduction**	
10 min.	**Taste Test**	p. 7
	SMART Goal Check-in	p. 11
5 min.	**Opening Question** *Do you notice a connection with how you feel and the foods you eat or how much you move your body? Describe a time when you noticed that.*	
15 min.	*Choose from the following:*	
	Activity Charades	IG p. 66
	» A game where participants identify sports and non-sports activities.	
	Thinking About Being Active	IG p. 106
	» Interactive group activity exploring the challenges and benefits of being active.	
	Make Moving Fun!	p. 62
	» Read a handout on the importance of daily exercise and discuss opportunities to get movement each day.	
10 min.	**Sleep Your Way to Health**	p. 65
	» A crossword puzzle about the importance of sleep.	
10 min.	**Healthy Changes**	p. 63
	» Strategize on ways to practice healthier eating with individual case studies.	
25 min.	**Recipe Demonstration or Activity (see EatFresh.org for ideas)**	
10 min.	**Post-workshop Questionnaire** Closing Question: *What is something you learned about yourself or how to do after attending this workshop?*	

Supplemental Handouts and Activities

» Weight and Body Size, p. 14

Setting the Stage for Healthy Habits // WEEK 1

Lesson Objective:
To consider personal ideas about food and health and look forward to a healthy life.

Time	Topics	Workbook Reference
15 min.	**Getting Started** Welcome and Introductions Pre-Workshop Survey (when applicable); Attendance	
10 min.	**Taste Test**	p. 7
5 min.	**Opening Question** *Why do you want to nourish and take care of your body? Besides eating nourishing food, what are other ways you can take care of your body?*	
10 min.	*Choose one:* **Food Collage** » Make a collage about health and nutritious food.	p. 8
	Your Healthy Life/Your Healthy Goals » Map out a healthy vision for the future then identify smaller steps that support the vision. Track progress each week.	p. 9-11
5 min.	**Kitchen Safety** » Participants learn the basics of kitchen safety.	p. 18*
15 min.	**Recipe Demonstration or Activity (see EatFresh.org for ideas)** » Choose a quick recipe for the first class. Closing Question: *What do you hope to learn in this class?*	

Supplemental Handouts and Activities

» How to Read a Recipe, p. 20

» Cooking with Eatfresh.org, p. 15*

» Measuring, IG p. 92

» Glossary of Recipe Terms, p. 19

» The Leah's Pantry DO EAT Food List, p. 12-13*

Building a Wholesome Diet // WEEK 2

Lesson Objective:
To learn some fundamentals of what types of foods make up a healthy diet.

Time	Topics	Workbook Reference
10 min.	**Welcome**	
	Taste Test	p. 7
5 min.	**Opening Question** *What does good nutrition mean to you or your family?*	
10 min.	**What's On MyPlate?**	p. 24-25
	» Read about MyPlate food groups and draw a MyPlate meal.	
15 min.	**My Family's Rainbow/Eat the Rainbow!**	p. 35-36
	» Categorize fruits and vegetables according to color and the nutrients they provide and determine which colors might be missing from the diet.	
20 min.	**Recipe Demonstration or Activity (see EatFresh.org for ideas)**	

Supplemental Handouts and Activities

» My Plate/Healthy Eating Plate, p. 26-27

» Food Group Bingo, p. 28

» Garden Sort, p. 42

» Setting the Table and Eating Together, p. 22*

» Food Journal (suggest participants complete this activity at home), p. 30

Lesson Objective:
To explore the spectrum of food processing and the advantages of eating whole foods.

Time	Topics	Workbook Reference
10 min.	**Welcome**	
	Taste Test	p. 7
5 min.	**Opening Question** *What are some of the reasons you eat fast or processed food or drink sugary beverages? What do you like about these items?*	
15 min.	*Choose from the following:*	
	Seed to Plant to Table	IG p. 101
	» Explore where different foods come from.	
	From Grain to Flour to Bread	IG p. 82
	» A hands-on experience of learning how grains become flour and the differences between whole wheat and white bread.	
	Grain Game, Bean Game	p. 38-41
	» Match grain and bean samples to their name and discuss possible ways of cooking each one.	
10 min.	**Food Processing**	p. 32-33
	» Read about different degrees of food processing and evaluate foods according to how processed they are.	
20 min.	**Recipe Demonstration or Activity (see EatFresh.org for ideas)**	
	Closing Question: *Do you notice a connection between different foods you eat and how you feel after eating them?*	

Supplemental Handouts and Activities

» Building Your Fire, p. 34

» Make Half Your Grains Whole, p. 37

» Plant Parts We Eat, p. 43

» Fuel Your Brain, p. 45*

Food Marketing // WEEK 4

Lesson Objective:
To become more aware of hidden marketing tactics and how to learn about hidden sugars from sugary drinks.

Time	Topics	Workbook Reference
10 min.	**Welcome**	
	Taste Test	p. 7
5 min.	**Opening Question** *How does advertising or what's on the package influence whether you buy or eat a product?*	
15 min.	**Food Marketing**	p. 59
	» Identify common tactics employed in food advertising to influence consumers.	
10 min.	**Rethink Your Drink**	p. 46-47
	» Guess the amount of sugar in various drinks and learn how to drink more water.	
20 min.	**Recipe Demonstration or Activity (see EatFresh.org for ideas)**	

Supplemental Handouts and Activities
» Nutrition Words to Know, p. 51

» Healthy Swaps, p. 50*

» Eating In-Season, p. 44*

» Creating a Recipe, IG p. 70

» Superstar Ingredients, p. 21*

» Don't Call Me Sugar! p. 48

» Eating Out and Staying Healthy, p. 64

Smart Shopping and Planning // WEEK 5

Lesson Objective:
To consider how food is marketed and develop skills for shopping and planning healthy meals.

Time	Topics	Workbook Reference
10 min.	**Welcome**	
	Taste Test	p. 7
5 min.	**Opening Question** *How do you help your family when it's time to buy groceries or plan a meal?*	
10 min.	**Make These Meals Healthier**	p. 29
	» Review sample meals and suggest ways of making them healthier.	
15 min.	**Anatomy of a Grocery Store/Outsmarting the Grocery Store**	p. 56-57
	» Participants map out their usual grocery store to indicate where the healthy food is placed, and discuss common supermarket tactics.	
	Creating a Meal Plan & Grocery List	p. 58
	» Practice meal planning and preparing a sample grocery list.	
20 min.	**Recipe Demonstration or Activity (see EatFresh.org for ideas)**	

Supplemental Handouts and Activities

» The Leah's Pantry DO EAT Food List, p. 12-13*

» Healthy Swaps, p. 50*

» Eating In-Season, p. 44*

» Creating a Recipe, IG p. 70

» Superstar ingredients, p. 21*

A Strong Body for Life // WEEK 6

Lesson Objective:
To explore holistic practices for good health.

Time	Topics	Workbook Reference
10 min.	**Welcome**	
	Taste Test	p. 7
5 min.	**Opening Question**	
	Do you notice a connection with how you feel and the foods you eat or how much you move your body? Describe a time when you noticed that.	
15 min.	*Choose from the following:*	
	Healthy Changes	p. 63
	» Strategize on ways to practice healthier eating with individual case studies.	
	Activity Charades	IG p. 66
	» A game where participants identify sports and non-sports activities.	
	Thinking About Being Active	IG p. 106
	» Interactive group activity exploring the challenges and benefits of being active.	
	Make Moving Fun!	p. 62
	» Read a handout on the importance of daily exercise and discuss opportunities to get movement each day.	
20 min.	**Recipe Demonstration or Activity (see EatFresh.org for ideas)**	
10 min.	**Post-workshop Questionnaire**	
	Closing Question: *What is something you learned about yourself or how to do after attending this workshop?*	

Supplemental Handouts and Activities

» Sleep Your Way to Health, p. 65

» Weight and Body Size, p. 14

Setting the Stage for Healthy Habits // WEEK 1

Lesson Objective:
To consider personal ideas about food and health and look forward to a healthy life.

Time	Topics	Workbook Reference
15 min.	**Getting Started** Welcome and Introductions Pre-Workshop Survey (when applicable); Attendance	
10 min.	**Taste Test**	p. 7
5 min	**Opening Question** *Why do you want to nourish and take care of your body? Besides eating nourishing food, what are other ways you can take care of your body?*	
15 min.	**Food Collage** » Make a collage about health and nutritious food.	p. 8
15 min.	**Your Healthy Life/Your Healthy Goals** » Map out larger health goals for the future as well as smaller steps that can be used to achieve that goal, and then track their progress.	p. 9-11
10 min.	**Kitchen Safety** » Participants learn the basics of kitchen safety.	p. 18*
20 min.	**Recipe Demonstration or Activity (see EatFresh.org for ideas)**	

Supplemental Handouts and Activities

» The Leah's Pantry DO EAT Food List, p. 12-13*

» How to Read a Recipe, p. 20

» Cooking with Eatfresh.org, p. 15*

» Measuring, IG p. 92

» Glossary of Recipe Terms, p. 19

Building a Wholesome Diet // WEEK 2

Lesson Objective:
To learn some fundamentals about what types of foods make up a healthy diet.

Time	Topics	Workbook Reference
5 min.	**Welcome and Introduction**	
10 min.	**Taste Test**	p. 7
	SMART Goal Check-in	p. 11
5 min.	**Opening Question**	
	What does good nutrition mean to you or your family?	
15 min.	**What's On MyPlate?**	p. 24-25
	» Read about MyPlate food groups and draw a MyPlate meal.	
15 min.	**My Family's Rainbow/Eat the Rainbow!**	p. 35-36
	» Categorize fruits and vegetables according to color and the nutrients they provide and determine which colors might be missing from the diet.	
15 min.	*Choose one of the following activities:*	
	Food Group Bingo	p. 28
	» Match foods to their corresponding food groups in a game of BINGO.	
	Healthy Hopscotch	IG p. 87
	» Play a game where foods are categorized into one of the 5 food groups	
	Restaurateur	IG p. 98
	» Invent a menu featuring creative uses of whole foods.	
25 min.	**Recipe Demonstration or Activity (see EatFresh.org for ideas)**	

Supplemental Handouts and Activities

» MyPlate/Healthy Eating Plate, p. 26-27

» Garden Sort, p. 42

» Fuel Your Brain, p. 45*

» Setting the Table and Eating Together, p. 22*

» Food Journal (suggest participants complete this activity at home), p. 30

Lesson Objective:
To explore the spectrum of food processing and the advantages of eating whole foods.

Time	Topics	Workbook Reference
5 min.	**Welcome and Introduction**	
10 min.	**Taste Test**	p. 7
	SMART Goal Check-in	p. 11
5 min.	**Opening Question**	
	What are some of the reasons you eat fast or processed food or drink sugary beverages? What do you like about these items?	
20 min.	*Choose from the following:*	
	Seed to Plant to Table	IG p. 101
	» Explore where different foods come from.	
	From Grain to Flour to Bread	IG p. 82
	» A hands-on experience of learning how grains become flour and the differences between whole wheat and white bread.	
	Grain Game, Bean Game	p. 38-41
	» Match grain and bean samples to their name and discuss possible ways of cooking each one.	
15 min.	**Food Processing**	p. 32-33
	» Read about different degrees of food processing and evaluate foods according to how processed they are.	
	Building Your Fire	p. 34
	» Name foods that fuel your body for a long time.	
10 min.	**Make These Meals Healthier**	p. 29
	» Review sample meals and suggest ways of making them healthier.	
25 min.	**Recipe Demonstration or Activity (see EatFresh.org for ideas)**	

Supplemental Handouts and Activities

» The Leah's Pantry DO EAT Food List, p. 12-13*

» Make Half Your Grains Whole, p. 37

» Plant Parts We Eat, p. 43

Lesson Objective:
To become more aware of hidden marketing tactics and how to learn about hidden sugars from sugary drinks.

Time	Topics	Workbook Reference
5 min.	**Welcome and Introduction**	
10 min.	**Taste Test**	p. 7
	SMART Goal Check-in	p. 11
5 min.	**Opening Question**	
	How does advertising or what's on the package influence whether you buy or eat a product?	
20 min.	**Don't Call Me Sugar!**	p. 48
	» Learn different terms for sugar with a word search.	
	Rethink Your Drink	p. 46-47
	» Guess the amount of sugar in various drinks and learn how to drink more water.	
15 min.	**Nutrition Words to Know**	p. 51
	» Learn about some of the nutrition terms found on a label by matching them with their definitions.	
	Food Labels—Nutrition Facts	p. 52-53
	» Identify and discuss key parts of the Nutrition Facts label.	
10 min.	**Food Marketing**	p. 59
	» Identify common tactics employed in food advertising to influence consumers.	
25 min.	**Recipe Demonstration or Activity (see EatFresh.org for ideas)**	

Supplemental Handouts and Activities

» Anatomy of a Grocery Store/Outsmarting the Grocery Store, p. 56-57

» Eating Out and Staying Healthy, p. 64

Lesson Objective:
To explore holistic practices for good health.

Time	Topics	Workbook Reference
5 min.	**Welcome and Introduction**	
10 min.	**Taste Test**	p. 7
	SMART Goal Check-in	p. 11
5 min.	**Opening Question** *Do you notice a connection with how you feel and the foods you eat or how much you move your body? Describe a time when you noticed that.*	
15 min.	*Choose from the following:*	
	Activity Charades	IG p. 66
	» A game where participants identify sports and non-sports activities.	
	Thinking About Being Active	IG p. 106
	» Interactive group activity exploring the challenges and benefits of being active.	
	Make Moving Fun!	p. 62
	» Read a handout on the importance of daily exercise and discuss opportunities to get movement each day.	
10 min.	**Sleep Your Way to Health**	p. 65
	» A crossword puzzle about the importance of sleep.	
10 min.	**Healthy Changes**	p. 63
	» Strategize on ways to practice healthier eating with individual case studies.	
25 min.	**Recipe Demonstration or Activity (see EatFresh.org for ideas)**	
10 min.	**Post-workshop Questionnaire** **Closing Question:** *What is something you learned about yourself or how to do after attending this workshop?*	

Supplemental Handouts and Activities

» Weight and Body Size, p. 14

Setting the Stage for Healthy Habits // WEEK 1

Lesson Objective:
To consider personal ideas about food and health and look forward to a healthy life.

Time	Topics	Workbook Reference
15 min.	**Getting Started** Welcome and Introductions Pre-Workshop Survey (when applicable); Attendance	
10 min.	**Taste Test**	p. 7
5 min.	**Opening Question** *Why do you want to nourish and take care of your body? Besides eating nourishing food, what are other ways you can take care of your body?*	
10 min.	*Choose one:* **Food Collage** » Make a collage about health and nutritious food.	p. 8
	Your Healthy Life/Your Healthy Goals » Map out a healthy vision for the future then identify smaller steps that support the vision. Track progress each week.	p. 9-11
5 min.	**Kitchen Safety** » Participants learn the basics of kitchen safety.	p. 18*
15 min.	**Recipe Demonstration or Activity (see EatFresh.org for ideas)** » Choose a quick recipe for the first class. **Closing Question:** *What do you hope to learn in this class?*	

Supplemental Handouts and Activities
» The Leah's Pantry DO EAT Food List, p. 12-13*
» How to Read a Recipe, p. 20
» Cooking with Eatfresh.org, p. 15*
» Measuring, IG p. 92
» Glossary of Recipe Terms, p. 19

Building a Wholesome Diet // WEEK 2

Lesson Objective:
To learn some fundamentals of what types of foods make up a healthy diet.

Time	Topics	Workbook Reference
10 min.	**Welcome**	
	Taste Test	p. 7
5 min.	**Opening Question** *What does good nutrition mean to you or your family?*	
10 min.	**What's On MyPlate?**	p. 24-25
	» Read about MyPlate food groups and draw a MyPlate meal.	
15 min.	**My Family's Rainbow/Eat the Rainbow!**	p. 35-36
	» Categorize fruits and vegetables according to color and the nutrients they provide and determine which colors might be missing from the diet.	
20 min.	**Recipe Demonstration or Activity (see EatFresh.org for ideas)**	

Supplemental Handouts and Activities

» My Plate/Healthy Eating Plate, p. 26-27

» Food Group Bingo, p. 28

» Garden Sort, p. 42

» Setting the Table and Eating Together, p. 22*

» Food Journal (suggest participants complete this activity at home), p. 30

58

© Copyright 2018-2022 Leah's Pantry Food Smarts Kids Instructor Guide

Lesson Objective:
To explore the spectrum of food processing and the advantages of eating whole foods.

Time	Topics	Workbook Reference
10 min.	**Welcome**	
	Taste Test	p. 7
5 min.	**Opening Question**	
	What are some of the reasons you eat fast or processed food or drink sugary beverages? What do you like about these items?	
15 min.	*Choose from the following:*	
	Seed to Plant to Table	IG p. 101
	» Explore where different foods come from.	
	From Grain to Flour to Bread	IG p. 82
	» A hands-on experience of learning how grains become flour and the differences between whole wheat and white bread.	
	Grain Game, Bean Game	p. 38-41
	» Match grain and bean samples to their name and discuss possible ways of cooking each one.	
10 min.	**Food Processing**	p. 32-33
	» Read about different degrees of food processing and evaluate foods according to how processed they are.	
20 min.	**Recipe Demonstration or Activity (see EatFresh.org for ideas)**	
	Closing Question: *Do you notice a connection between different foods you eat and how you feel after eating them?*	

Supplemental Handouts and Activities

» Building Your Fire, p. 34

» Make Half Your Grains Whole, p. 37

» Plant Parts We Eat, p. 43

» Fuel Your Brain, p. 45*

Lesson Objective:

To become more aware of hidden marketing tactics and how to learn about hidden sugars from sugary drinks.

Time	Topics	Workbook Reference
10 min.	**Welcome** **Taste Test**	 p. 7
5 min.	**Opening Question** *How does advertising or what's on the package influence whether you buy or eat a product?*	
15 min.	**Food Marketing** » Identify common tactics employed in food advertising to influence consumers.	p. 59
10 min.	**Rethink Your Drink** » Guess the amount of sugar in various drinks and learn how to drink more water.	p. 46-47
20 min.	**Recipe Demonstration or Activity (see EatFresh.org for ideas)**	

Supplemental Handouts and Activities

» Nutrition Words to Know, p. 51

» Anatomy of a Grocery Store/Outsmarting the Grocery Store, p. 56-57

» Eating Out and Staying Healthy, p. 64

» Don't Call Me Sugar! p. 48

A Strong Body for Life // WEEK 5

Lesson Objective:
To explore holistic practices for good health.

Time	Topics	Workbook Reference
10 min.	**Welcome**	
	Taste Test	p. 7
5 min.	**Opening Question** *Do you notice a connection with how you feel and the foods you eat or how much you move your body? Describe a time when you noticed that.*	
15 min.	*Choose from the following:*	
	Healthy Changes	p. 63
	» Strategize on ways to practice healthier eating with individual case studies.	
	Activity Charades	IG p. 66
	» A game where participants identify sports and non-sports activities.	
	Thinking About Being Active	IG p. 106
	» Interactive group activity exploring the challenges and benefits of being active.	
	Make Moving Fun!	p. 62
	» Read a handout on the importance of daily exercise and discuss opportunities to get movement each day.	
20 min.	**Recipe Demonstration or Activity (see EatFresh.org for ideas)**	
10 min.	**Post-workshop Questionnaire** Closing Question: *What is something you learned about yourself or how to do after attending this workshop?*	

Supplemental Handouts and Activities

» Sleep Your Way to Health, p. 65

» Weight and Body Size, p. 14

Objectives

» Participants are introduced to EatFresh.org and the EatFresh.org Mini Course as trusted and easy-to-use online resources for recipes and health information.

» Participants practice digital literacy skills, such as creating an online account and navigating through an online course.

» Participants increase their knowledge and confidence in making healthy dietary choices.

Materials

» computers or tablets

» projector and screen (optional)

» headphones/earbuds

» butcher paper or white board (optional)

Preparation

1. If using a projector, connect it to a computer and open EatFresh.org in a browser, like Chrome.

2. Open a clean browser on all computers in the lab. Use Chrome if possible.

3. Write the opening questions on the butcher paper:

    » What is one tip you have for living a healthy life?

    » What is one challenge you have in living a healthy life?

Agenda

10 min Introduction

10 min Overview of EatFresh.org

15 min EatFresh.org Mini Course Account Creation

20 min Referral Code, Check-in Questionnaire, and Introduction to the EatFresh.org Mini Course

5 min Closing

Introduction

1. Greet participants by learning their name and whether they use the computer frequently. Seat users with the least computer experience near your computer, or pair them with more experienced users.

2. Briefly introduce yourself to the class and give an overview of the topics to be discussed today.

3. In groups of 2–3, have participants introduce themselves by answering questions on the butcher paper (if using) or read them out loud. If the group is small, this can be done as a whole group.

4. After a few minutes, ask each group to briefly share highlights and record their answers on the butcher paper (if using). Use ++ to show agreement.

5. Summarize the main bright spots and the main difficulties of the group. Make sure to address these during the course of the series.

EatFresh.org Overview

EatFresh.org is a website for anyone who wants to eat and live healthy on a budget. EatFresh.org can be used whenever you have internet access. It is an easy way to find health information and good recipes.

Features Overview

Review each main section of EatFresh.org in the main menu by hovering over the main sections of the site on the projector (if using) or point them out on participants' devices.

1. **Find a Recipe**—search by keyword or filter over 500 low cost, healthy recipes; find suggested meal plans on EatFresh.org for groups of recipes that help to reduce food waste and cost.

2. **Ask a Dietitian**—submit a question to the online dietitian or read answers to others' questions.

3. **Find Farmers' Markets & Get Help Putting Food on the Table**—these link to external resources for finding farmers' markets that accept EBT (food stamps) and information about EBT programs in California.

1. **Discover Foods**—learn more about specific foods or food groups, such as how to cook it, store it, and why it's good for our bodies.

2. **Cultivate a Healthy Lifestyle**—find tips and resources for cooking, nutrition, physical activity, chronic disease prevention, and more.

Have each participant click on "Recipes" and find one recipe they think looks tasty. Encourage participants to use the recipe filters or search for a food that they like for more ideas on how to enjoy it. Share it with a partner. If the group is more advanced, have them text or e-mail the recipe they chose to themselves or post it on social media.

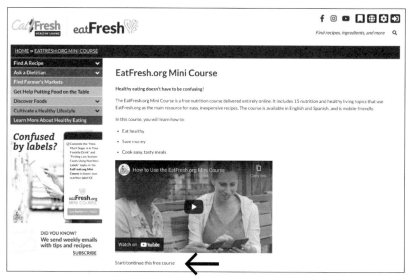

Figure 1. EatFresh.org Mini Course Link

EatFresh.org Mini Course Account Creation and Referral Code

1. Ask each participant to return to the EatFresh.org homepage and click on the **EatFresh.org Mini Course** link at the bottom of the page. Then, click on **Start/continue this free course** (Figure 1) to switch to the EatFresh.org learning management system. (Participants can bookmark the resulting page to easily return to it later.)

2. Read steps 1-5, then click the **Signup** button (Figure 2).

3. Participants will be asked to enter their name and e-mail address, and choose a username and password. (Figure 3) *Ask participants to write down their login credentials on an EatFresh.org recipe card, in a note app on their phone, or model it after username and passwords they have for other online accounts. While this suggestion isn't a recommended strategy for accounts storing sensitive personal data, like banking websites, it can be ok for our EatFresh.org Mini Course site.*

4. The sign up area also prompts participants to enter a referral code if they have received one. *Referral codes are optional and allow us to track who is using the EatFresh.org Mini Course. We can then share your participant's data for your own reporting purposes. Request a referral code by e-mailing products@leahspantry.org.*

Figure 2. EatFresh.org Learning Management System

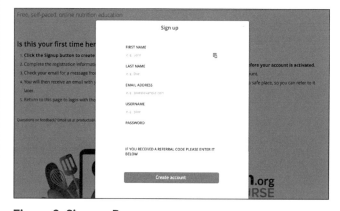

Figure 3. Sign-up Pop-up

Figure 4. Login Button

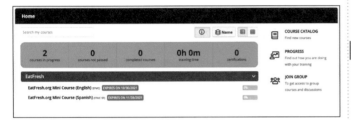

Figure 5. Learner Home

1. Next, participants will be sent a verification e-mail letting them know their account on the learning management system is ready. Ask them to check their e-mail and click the **Confirm your account** link.

2. Return to the login page and select the orange **Login** button (Figure 4).

3. Once logged in, participants will find a personalized dashboard where progress is tracked. (Figure 5) The EatFresh.org Mini Course is available in English and Spanish. Participants can select the course with their preferred language and begin their training.

Check-in Questionnaire, and Introduction to the EatFresh.org Mini Course

1. Next, ask participants to fill out the Demographic Questions and complete the EatFresh.org Mini Course Check-in Questionnaire.

2. Start the course! Topics can be taken in any order. Ask participants to complete 1-2 topics. As they go through the topics, assist participants in troubleshooting problems and answer any questions that come up.

3. Encourage participants to complete the remaining topics on their own time. Once the first five topics have been completed, participants will be asked to complete the Nutrition Basics Follow-up Questionnaire.

4. After Modules 1-5 and the related questionnaire have been completed, users can view their certificate of completion. If you are able to, offer an incentive that can be earned by showing you their certificate of completion. *Certificates of completion can be found in the dropdown menu at the top of the page, under My Certifications, and can be downloaded or shared to LinkedIn.*

Closing

1. Have everyone turn their attention to the group, and ask each person to **share one thing they learned or a healthy change they would like to make this week**.

2. Thank them for participating and remind them that they can return to the EatFresh.org Mini Course to complete the other topics, or re-watch them as many times as they would like, for 90 days. They can also visit EatFresh.org for recipes, health tips, and county resources.

Activities

Activity Charades

All Ages

A game where participants identify sports and non-sports activities for staying active on a daily basis.

Materials

» paper and pen

» stopwatch, clock, or wristwatch

Desired Outcomes

» Participants identify a variety of ways to be active.

» Participants identify physical activity with activities other than exercise or working out.

» Participants identify factors that make exercise difficult to fit in, and then potential solutions.

Directions

1. If there are more than 6 students, divide the class into two teams. Otherwise, avoid a competition and just play with the whole group together.

2. Have each team brainstorm different ways to be active (i.e. rock climbing, soccer, dance, cooking, running). Encourage the participants to include activities that are active, but not sports (i.e. cleaning the house, carrying groceries, climbing stairs). Each team should write these ideas on slips of paper and give them to the opposite team. If working with kids who cannot yet write, have one child who can, do the writing for them.

3. If you are playing with one team, have each participant think of an idea on their own and act it out. You can assist kids who are having trouble.

4. One player from each team takes a slip of paper and attempts to get their team to guess the activity. Each time a player acts out a phrase, a stopwatch is used to track the time (with a maximum of two minutes for each turn). The team with the least amount of total minutes and seconds wins. For a group of younger students, you may need to whisper ideas into their ears and avoid the stopwatch.

5. Extension: Play again using the question: "What are things that prevent people from exercising every day?" (i.e. TV, being tired, homework, nothing to do, etc.)

Discussion Questions

» What were some ideas that you hadn't thought of on your own?

» Do you prefer being physically active with other people or on your own?

» Why is being active an important part of a healthy life?

» Why is being active every day challenging? What gets in the way?

Adapting for Younger Kids

Have the whole group stand in an open area, ideally in a circle if space allows. Choose a familiar activity to act out, such as swimming, dancing, or riding a bicycle. Have kids guess what you are modeling and then imitate you. After a few rounds, invite volunteers to take turns choosing and acting out their own favorite activities for classmates to imitate.

Anatomy of a Grocery Store/Outsmarting the Grocery Store   *Ages 9+*

Participants map out their usual grocery store to indicate where the healthy food is placed, and discuss common supermarket tactics.

◼ Materials

Pick and choose depending on the variation:

» workbook pages p. 56-57

» paper and pen; magazines (option one)

» food, food models or food cards (option two)

◼ Desired Outcomes

» Participants build awareness of how grocery stores are laid out and how that may influence their choices.

» Participants identify ways in which they can navigate the grocery story, outsmart marketing tactics, and save money.

◼ Directions

Option One—Creating a Grocery Store Map

Using the blank paper, markers and magazines, have the participants label the different parts of the grocery store and paste pictures of appropriate foods on their map. The main idea with this activity is that participants become aware of where the whole foods are (usually on the perimeter) and where the processed foods are (usually in the aisles).

This activity is appropriate when there isn't enough space or there are too many participants to do Option Two.

Knowledge of the local grocery stores is important here—try to visit the store most of the participants frequent.

Option Two—Creating a Grocery Store in the Classroom

This option works well if you have a limited number of participants and a dedicated space for class with chairs and tables that can be moved around. Set up the classroom to be a "grocery store" and lay out ingredients used in the weekly recipe and/or food cards. Take the participants on a "tour" of the grocery store, highlighting the perimeter vs. the aisles. Have them shop for their recipe. Introduce some of the tricks of the grocer detailed on the next page.

This is a difficult activity to attempt with a large number of participants or if you have a limited amount of space.

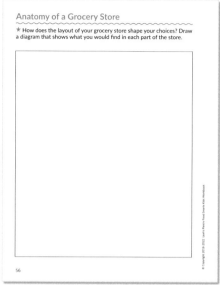

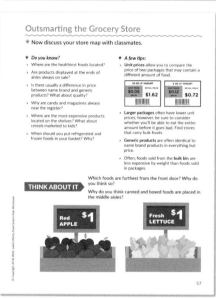

[continues on next page...]

▊ Discussion Questions

Discuss these questions as a whole group or in pairs.

Where are the healthiest foods located?

» Around the perimeter (along the 4 walls) of the store: dairy, produce and fresh meat.

» The foods located in the aisles are often highly processed foods that contain high percentages of preservatives, fat, salt, or sugar that can make you sick. Are products displayed at the ends of aisles on sale?

» Not usually—and they're often products that don't match the products in the aisles. They're often designed to be an impulse purchase and you will buy it simply because you are walking by.

Is there usually a difference in price between name brand and store-brand products? What about quality?

» Store-brand products are usually cheaper, although always watch for sales!

» Quality is often the same, but exceptions apply.

Why are candy and magazines always near the register?

» People are more likely to make an impulse purchase and buy something that's right where they are standing.

» These are items that stores make more money from.

Where are most expensive products located on the shelves? What about cereals marketed to kids?

» Most expensive products are at eye-level, cheaper products are higher and lower.

» Kids cereals are the most expensive at kids' eye-level.

When should you put refrigerated and frozen foods in your cart? Why?

» Frozen and refrigerated goods should be placed in the cart at the end of your shopping trip, so as to limit the amount of time they are out of the refrigerator or freezer.

Creating a Meal Plan and Grocery List

Practice meal planning and preparing a sample grocery list.

Materials

» workbook p. 58

» pen

Desired Outcomes

» Participants learn how to create a grocery list from a meal plan.

» Participants consider the advantages of planning and list making.

Directions

» Using the worksheet, ask participants to plan two meals for their family. Then, create a grocery list from those dishes. Use the example on the worksheet to explain how it is done.

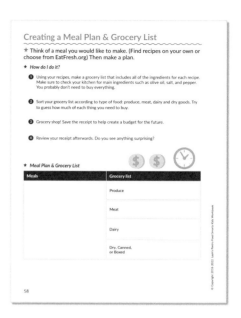

Discussion Questions

» What are the advantages of planning and making grocery lists?

  » ingredients (especially produce items) can be used in multiple recipes, which eliminates waste

  » food purchased is consumed during the week

  » last minute shopping at higher priced convenience stores is eliminated

  » less time and energy is spent wondering what's for dinner!

  » kids can help with the planning, making them more likely to eat the meals that are prepared

» When you make a grocery list at home, what kinds of things do you have to think about in order to make this list?

EatFresh.org Integration

Look up "Shopping & Budgeting" pages under the Cultivate A Healthy Lifestyle tab on EatFresh.org. Ask participants to share a new tip they learned from these pages.

Creating a Recipe

Ages 8+

Participants create and share a recipe from scratch.

Materials

» paper and pencils

Desired Outcomes

» Participants reinforce their knowledge of reading recipes by creating original recipes.

» Participants experiment and get creative with cooking.

Directions

1. First, ask participants to consider the following questions:

     » What are the parts of a recipe?

     » Do you have any favorite recipes? What are they?

     » Where do recipes come from? Who invents recipes?

     » Do you know people who cook without a recipe?

2. Next, give participants free reign to write a recipe for anything they choose. If you like, brainstorm ideas together as a class beforehand. Encourage participants to think about foods they like to eat and to come up with an original dish or simple snack based on this. Or they can try to write down a dish they prepare or have seen someone else prepare. If participants are stuck on figuring out how much of an ingredient to use, encourage them to use their best guess, and remind them that all recipes begin as experiments!

3. When everyone has finished writing a recipe, invite participants to read their recipes to the group. Encourage participants to share their recipes with their parents and to try making them together at home.

© Copyright 2018-2022 Leah's Pantry Food Smarts Kids Instructor Guide

Don't Call Me Sugar!

Ages 9+

Learn different terms for sugar with a word search.

▍ Materials

» workbook page p. 48

» paper and pen

» various labels containing different types of sugar

▍ Desired Outcomes:

» Participants can recognize different forms of sugar in their food.

▍ Directions

1. Have participants complete the "Sugar Word Search."

   » **Read the ingredients list.** Learn to identify terms that mean sugar, including sugar, white sugar, brown sugar, confectioner's sugar, corn syrup, dextrin, honey, invert sugar, maple syrup, raw sugar, beet sugar, cane sugar, corn sweeteners, evaporated cane juice, high fructose corn syrup, malt, molasses, turbinado sugar, sorbitol, aspartame, dextrose, sweetener, glucose, saccharin, fructose, maltose, nutrasweet, and lactose.

2. Have each student read three labels, listing all the forms of sugar found in each food.

   » It can be confusing to try to find out how much added sugar a food contains. The sugar listing on a Nutrition Facts label lumps all sugars together, including naturally-occurring milk and fruit sugars, which can be deceiving. This explains why, according to the label, one cup of milk has 11 grams of sugar even though it doesn't contain any sugar "added" to it.

▍ Discussion Questions

» Why is having different names for sugar confusing?

» What are some examples of food that have naturally-occurring sugars?

Eating Out and Staying Healthy

Read about strategies for healthier choices when dining out and brainstorm ways to balance out fast-food or restaurant meals.

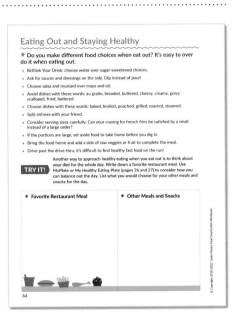

Materials

» workbook p. 64

Desired Outcome

» Participants identify strategies for healthier decision-making when eating out.

» Participants identify ways to balance out their overall diet for the day when some of their meals are eaten out.

Directions

1. Have participants reflect for a moment to identify how many meals they get each week from restaurants (including fast-food establishments). It is not necessary to ask participants to share this information.

2. Read the tips listed in the workbook together and ask participants to share if there are any listed that they practice.

3. Read the tips listed in the workbook together and ask participants to share if there are any listed that they practice.

4. Have participants write down a typical meal they might eat out. Then they can identify what choices they can make during other parts of the day so they can have a balanced diet through out the day. Have they refer to MyPlate or Healthy Eating plate for ideas for things they can incorporate so they can obtain important nutrients.

Discussion Questions

» What is challenging about making healthy decisions when you eat out?

» Are there any places you and your family like to eat that have healthy choices easier? Why?

» Which of the tips listed would you like to try?

Facilitation Tips

» Reinforce that eating out often may lead us to consume high amounts of fat, salt, and sugar. Home prepared meals allow you more control over what goes into your body. But we can still have a healthy diet even if we choose to eat out.

» Remember not to demonize certain kinds of foods or sources of meals. Fast food and eating out are a part of many people's lives and can be a way to celebrate, connect with others, or do something special for oneself or a loved one.

72

Food Collage

Make a collage about health and nutritious food.

Materials

- » workbook p. 8
- » magazines or grocery flyers
- » scissors
- » glue sticks
- » markers/crayons
- » large paper

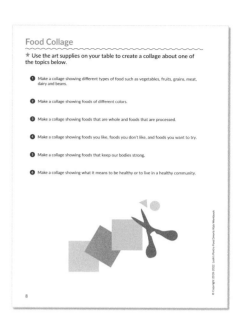

Desired Outcomes

- » Participants creatively share their knowledge about food, nutrition and health.

Directions

1. Give each student a piece of paper and access to markers/crayons, glue sticks, magazine/grocery inserts, and scissors.

2. Depending on the age and knowledge of the group, have them choose one of the collage options, or choose one fore them.

3. Depending on time and the size of the class, have participants present their collages to the class.

Discussion Questions

- » Why do you like the foods you put on your list? Reasons might be because they taste good, are healthy, are what you're used to eating, etc.

- » What are some different reasons we eat?

- » What foods would you like to try in this class?

Food Marketing

Identify common tactics employed in food advertising to influence consumers.

Materials

» workbook p. 59

» printed and laminated examples of food ads from social media, internet, magazines

Desired Outcome

» Participants recognize strategies that food marketers use to sell their products.

» Participants become more aware of how they might be influenced by advertisements without knowing.

Directions

1. Pass out the laminated ads. As a class, read the marketing tactics listed in the workbook.

2. Ask participants to identify examples of these tactics in the printed ads or others they might have seen.

Discussion Questions

» Do you ever notice how advertisers try to get your attention or influence you to buy their products?

» Have you ever had the desire to buy or eat a product from the way the packaging or advertisement is designed?

» What are the ways your beliefs or attitudes about a product might be affected by marketing strategies.

Food Group Bingo

All Ages

Match foods to their corresponding food groups in a game of BINGO.

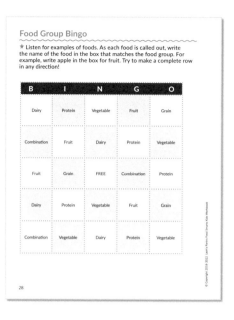

Materials

» workbook p. 28

» paper and pencils

» examples of foods (pictures or actual food items), or a list of various foods

Desired Outcomes

» Participants test their ability to identify the foods that are in each food group.

Directions

1. Have participants open workbooks to the Food Group Bingo sheet.

2. Randomly select a food item, and either call out the name or show participants the picture or item.

3. Ask participants to identify the food.

4. Have participants write the name of the food in one of the squares for that food group on their cards. For example, if a muffin is shown, participants write 'muffin' in one of the Grain Group squares. Let participants know they don't have to worry about correct spelling.

5. The first player to fill five squares horizontally, vertically or diagonally wins.

6. As a check, have the winner read off the names in the winning food/food group squares.

7. To play more than one round, have participants write the name of the food you mention in the top left corner of each box; in later rounds, have them write food named in the bottom right.

Food Journal

Ages 9+

A one day food journal and reflection on eating patterns and their interaction with our lives.

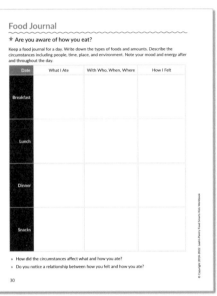

Materials

» workbook p. 30

» pens

Desired Outcomes

» Participants record and analyze a day of meals to discover how various circumstances might affect their eating.

» Participants reflect on how food can impact their mood and energy.

Directions

1. Ask participants to keep a journal of what they ate for a day. Alternatively, you can ask them to recall the previous day but it may be less accurate.

2. Explain to participants that the purpose of this activity is to bring some awareness to our eating habits, but it is not meant to be a way to "diet" or judge what we eat. Instead, being aware is the first step to finding healthful and balanced ways to nourishing ourselves.

3. Emphasize that food marketing, the environment, location, hunger levels, time, mood, and availability of food play a big part in what and how we eat in ways we may not realize.

Discussion Questions

» What was challenging about keeping the journal? Was it easy or helpful in any way?

» How did the circumstances affect what and how you ate? What made it easier to eat in a balanced way? What made it harder?

» What surprised you?

» Were there meals that helped improve your mood or energy?

» What are some things in this journal that you want to change or continue or do more often to support balanced eating?

Facilitation Tips

» Allow participants to share what they feel comfortable with. Some may feel uncomfortable sharing too many details about their eating habits. Encourage them to make their own notes and reflections in their workbook for their own understanding.

» Encourage participants to be curious about what and why they eat rather than judge themselves for eating the right or wrong things.

» Encourage participants to identify things they are proud of in their journal.

» Reinforce that it may be helpful for some people to occasionally write down or track their eating patterns but not something necessary or even ideal to do over the long term.

Food Labels—Nutrition Facts

Identify and discuss key parts of the Nutrition Facts label.

Materials

» workbook p. 52-53

» several examples of nutrition labels on food packaging (Actual food packaging is better than a print out of a nutrition label.)

» a set of measuring cups: 1 c, ½ c, ⅓ c, ¼ c

Outcomes

» Participants can identify where serving size, calories, sodium, saturated fat, and ingredients are located on the nutrition label.

» Participants learn what each category means.

Directions

1. Explain: Knowing how to read the nutrition facts label is very useful for being a smart and healthy shopper. It presents a lot of information and every food is required to use the same format so you can compare easily.

2. Discuss each category on the label.

Serving Size

» Ask participants to find the "serving size" on the nutrition label.

» All the nutritional information on the label is all based on the measurement of a serving size. The nutritional information on the label is all based on this measurement. Example: ¼ cup is the serving size of this product. All the other information (the amount of sugars, fat, calories, etc.) corresponds to this amount of food.

» Ask: Does this seem like a reasonable serving size? If you were to eat this food, how many serving sizes would you eat at one time?

Calories

» Ask participants to find "calories" on the nutrition label.

» Calories are a measurement of energy that can be used when eating a food product. Eating more calories than what your body burns naturally and from moving can lead to weight gain. Eating too few calories can lead to low energy, mood, and loss of muscle.

» We need approximately 2,000 calories per day, but the total depends on various factors such as age, body size, and activity levels.

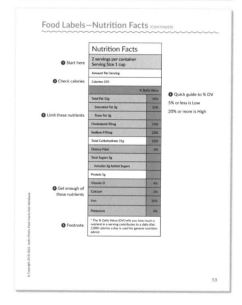

[continues on next page...]

Food Labels—Nutrition Facts (CONTINUED)

Sodium

» Ask participants to find "sodium" on the nutrition label.

» Limit sodium intake to <2,300 mg/day (no hypertension), <1500 mg/day (with hypertension).

» Eating too much sodium may increase risk for chronic disease such as hypertension and stroke.

» Ask: What are some foods you eat that are high in sodium? Do you often salt your food?

Saturated Fats & Trans Fats

» Ask participants to identify "saturated fat" on the nutrition label.

» Aim for foods that are close to 5% or less.

» Eating too much saturated fat may increase risk for chronic disease like cardiovascular disease.

» Many times the nutrition label will show "0g" for Trans Fat, but you will notice "partially hydrogenated corn oil" (or similar) in the ingredient list. This means that for a single serving size, there is less than 1g. It does not mean there are no trans fats in the product.

Ingredient list

» Ask participants to find the "ingredient list" on the food product.

» The first ingredient listed is the most abundant.

» If sugar is the first ingredient, then the product is probably not one you want to eat a lot of to be healthy.

» Look for "whole wheat" or another whole grain to be first on the list if you are looking for whole grain foods. "Wheat flour" does not mean "whole wheat."

» Ideally, choose foods with short ingredient lists where you recognize the words.

Food Label Scavenger Hunt

Compare and analyze two Nutrition Facts labels to determine the healthier choice.

▊ Materials

» workbook p. 54

▊ Desired Outcomes

» Participants recognize parts of a nutrition label.

» Participants use their knowledge to draw conclusions about the healthfulness of two food products.

» Participants compare saturated fat, vitamin content, and fiber on different food labels.

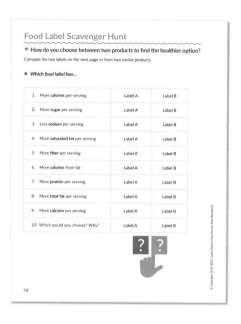

▊ Directions

1. If they haven't completed it yet, have participants do "Nutrition Words To Know" on p. 51. Use the handouts to help. Serving size will be covered in more depth during a later session, but be sure to use this as an opportunity to introduce the topic.

2. Follow directions on the Food Label Scavenger Hunt page.

▊ Discussion Questions

» How can food labels help us decide which foods to buy?

» Are food labels confusing?

» What kind of information do you or your family look for on a food label?

» What kind of food do you think the sample labels come from? (granola bars) Which would you choose?

Food Processing

Ages 9+

Read about different degrees of food processing and evaluate foods according to how processed they are.

Materials

» workbook p. 32-33

» examples of foods in various stages of processing (i.e. fresh apple, apple sauce, apple-flavored fruit snacks)

Desired Outcomes

» Participants consider the differences between "whole foods," "minimally processed," and "ultra processed" foods.

» Participants identify reasons why whole foods and minimally processed foods are healthier for themselves and our environment.

Directions

1. Line up the food samples from least processed to most processed. Ask participants what the differences are between these foods and consider how various foods are made.

   » How are they made?

   » Could they be made at home? How many ingredients does each have?

   » How are bread and cereal made? Soft drinks? Hot chips?

2. Read the headnotes on page 33. Have participants complete the activity.

3. Discuss benefits of Whole foods:

   » original nutrients--especially vitamins, minerals, and fiber are intact

   » nothing added - no salt, sugar, chemicals, colorings, etc. Commercially processed foods often add these things to improve appearance, flavor or texture that gets lost in the processing.

   » less processing means less energy to produce = better for the earth

   » less processing usually means less packaging = less waste

   » fresh taste

4. How are ultra processed foods different from whole or minimally processed foods?

   » Highly processed foods often require a factory or lab to produce and their raw ingredients are hard to identify.

   » They are often so highly processed that nutrients have to be added back because they were lost along the way.

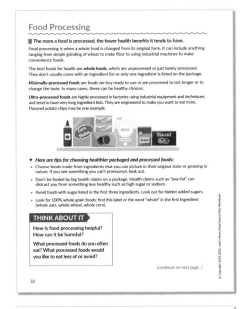

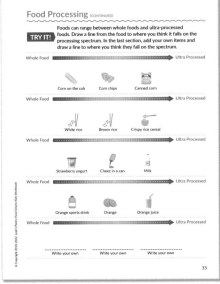

Food Processing (CONTINUED)

» Ultra processed foods tend to be higher in salt, added sugars and less healthy fats than whole foods. Some highly processed foods contain flavor enhancers that can encourage eating past fullness.

» Many whole or minimally processed foods are rich in fiber, protein and healthy fats and can be more satiating than ultra processed foods.

5. Optional: Have participants complete the Building Your Fire activity on the next page.

▌Discussion Questions

» Why are foods are processed?

  » Foods last longer.

  » Taste, convenience, timesaving.

  » Make it more marketable, create variety.

  » Some light processing can help make a food more digestible or nutritious.

» Turning ingredients into something else is considered processing. What are examples of processing that you can do at home?

  » Chopping, heating, baking, canning, freezing, drying.

» What are ways you use minimally-processed foods to create balanced meals at home?

From Grain to Flour to Bread

A hands-on experience of learning how grains become flour and the differences between whole wheat and white bread.

■ Materials

- » ½ cup of whole intact grain (i.e. wheat berries, oat groats, farro, rye berries)

- » small samples of whole wheat and wheat flour

- » an electric coffee grinder (optional)

- » tasting samples of whole wheat bread and white bread

■ Desired Outcomes

- » Participants learn about how grains are processed to make flour.

■ Directions

1. Display a sample of whole intact grain in an unmarked container or baggie. Have participants observe the grain up close with a magnifying glass, if possible. Can they identify what it is? Explain: this is what our favorite white bread, noodles, and cakes are usually made from!

2. Then display unmarked samples of white flour and whole wheat flour. Again, ask participants to observe and guess what these are.

3. Finally, explain how the flours are made by grinding the wheat berries and, in the case of white flour, removing some parts. If you have an electric coffee grinder, show participants grind some of the grains into flour.

4. Provide small samples of 100% whole wheat bread vs. soft white bread to taste test. Encourage participants to observe that the white bread has less taste and texture than the whole wheat because some parts have been removed.

■ Discussion Questions

- » Which do you think takes the most work for your body to break down?

- » Which do you think has the most nutrients in it? The least? Why?

Garden Sort

Sort vegetables according to how they grow.

▮ Materials

» workbook p. 42

» optional: a printed or online encyclopedia with information about edible plants

▮ Desired Outcomes

» Participants learn about plant foods and how they grow.

▮ Directions

1. Work though the sorting activity as a whole group or in pairs/small groups.

2. Have participants give examples of other plant foods, not shown, that could go in each category. (For example, apples grow on trees, potatoes grow underground, etc.)

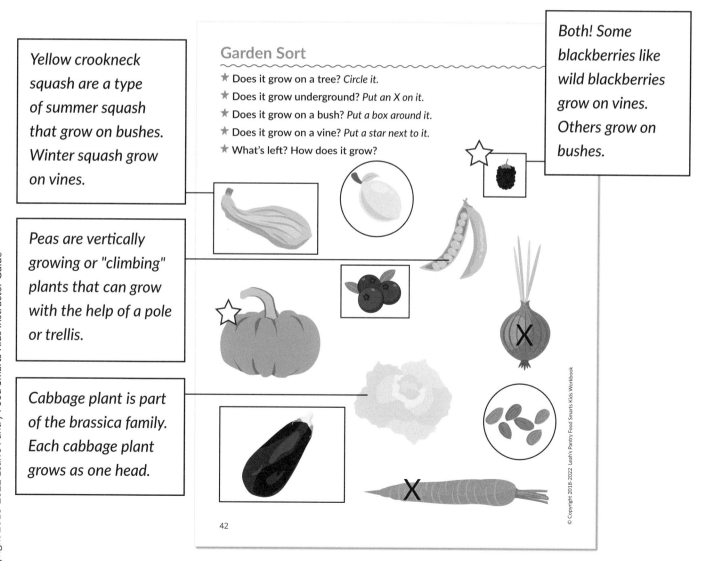

Yellow crookneck squash are a type of summer squash that grow on bushes. Winter squash grow on vines.

Peas are vertically growing or "climbing" plants that can grow with the help of a pole or trellis.

Cabbage plant is part of the brassica family. Each cabbage plant grows as one head.

Garden Sort

★ Does it grow on a tree? *Circle it.*
★ Does it grow underground? *Put an X on it.*
★ Does it grow on a bush? *Put a box around it.*
★ Does it grow on a vine? *Put a star next to it.*
★ What's left? How does it grow?

Both! Some blackberries like wild blackberries grow on vines. Others grow on bushes.

42

Glossary of Recipe Terms

Identify common words used in recipes by matching cooking terms with their definitions.

Materials

» workbook p. 19

» pens

Desired Outcomes

» Participants learn common recipe terms.

Directions

» Have participants work independently, in pairs, or as a whole group to complete the matching activity.

Discussion Questions

» Which words were new to you?

» Are there any other recipe words you'd like to learn about? (If time allows, have the group look at EatFresh.org for ideas. Then work together to find definitions on the internet.)

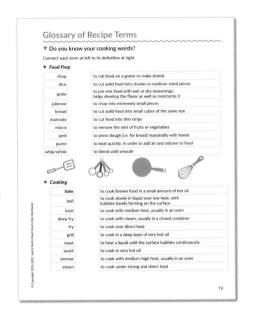

Grain Game, Bean Game *All Ages*

Match grain and bean samples to their name and discuss possible ways of cooking each one.

Materials

» small amount of each grain and bean in individual, small, numbered baggies (suggested)

» workbook p. 38-41

» pens

Desired Outcomes

» Participants explore the traditional uses of a variety of whole grains and beans.

Directions

1. In working pairs, have participants pass around the bag and try to identify the names of each food by placing the corresponding number from the baggie in the space provided on the workbook page.

2. Alternatively, participants can match the images on the second page with the correct name.

3. Have them read out loud about a bean or grain they might want to learn more about.

Discussion questions

» Which of these are you familiar with? How do you prepare it? Is there a recipe or dish your family traditionally prepares?

» Which one is new to you?

» Which one would you like to try? How could you prepare it?

Healthy Changes

Strategize on ways to practice healthier eating with individual case studies.

....

Materials

» workbook p. 63

Desired Outcomes

» Participants apply information they have learned to realistic scenarios in order to make holistic dietary changes.

Directions

1. Break the class up into groups of two or three.

2. Read the scenario out loud and have the participants respond to the question on the page.

3. Bring the class back together and discuss each group's suggestions.

Discussion Questions

» Did you identify with any of the people in the case studies?

» How would you write your story as a scenario like this?

» What changes might you make to your habits based on this activity?

» Which aspects of your routine do you want to keep?

Healthy Hopscotch

Play a game where foods are categorized into one of the 5 food groups

▮ Materials

» sidewalk chalk

» bean bag or some other object to throw on the hopscotch board

▮ Desired Outcomes

» Participants can correctly categorize different foods.

▮ Directions

1. Draw a large hopscotch board with sidewalk chalk and write the name of one food group in each square.

2. A player throws a beanbag or other small marker onto a square. Before the player hops, s/he must name a food from that food group.

3. The player continues from square to square, naming foods for the indicated food group until the course is completed.

4. If an incorrect answer is given, the player gets a second chance after the next student takes a turn.

5. Award everyone with fruit as a prize or a piece of sidewalk chalk.

How to Read a Recipe

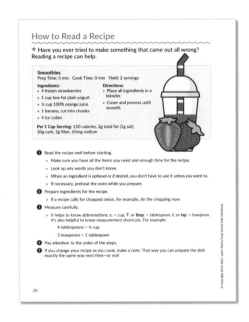

Learn to read a recipe accurately for successful cooking.

Materials

» workbook p. 20

» EatFresh.org or Leah's Pantry recipe booklet

Desired Outcomes

» Participants identify the parts of a recipe.

» Participants are able to double a recipe.

» Participants identify ingredients that may be swapped for others in some recipes.

Directions

1. Explain that a recipe is like a map, and that it is helpful to read the entire recipe before beginning so you know where to go!

2. Have participants read through each step of "How to Read a Recipe."

3. Using this session's recipe or the sample provided read through the recipe as a class, making a note of the title, ingredient list, directions, yield, and other information provided.

4. Ask participants to double the recipe. Have the participants figure out the measurements needed to double how much is made.

5. Explain that sometimes ingredients can be switched, and that these tricks can be helpful in a pinch or to make a recipe healthier. Review a few basic ingredient swaps by clicking on an ingredient on a recipe or searching for an ingredient in the "Discover Foods" page on eatfresh.org

Make Half Your Grains Whole

All Ages

Explore the differences between whole grains and refined grains and determine which products are a source of whole grains.

Materials

» workbook p. 37

» package samples from products that contain grains, including some whole grain products

Desired Outcomes

» Participants identify some differences between whole grains and refined grains.

» Participants learn some benefits of consuming whole grains.

» Participants practice using food labels to identify whole grain products.

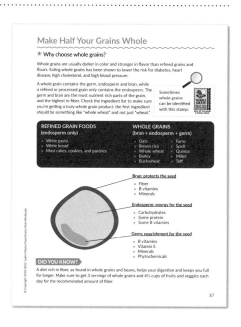

Directions

1. Review the handout and diagram with the whole group.

2. Pass out the packaging samples to individuals or pairs.

3. Explain that they should try to find products that have whole grains as a first ingredient. These usually have "whole" or "whole grain" in the name, such as "whole wheat" or "whole grain oats."

4. Note any products that might have the whole grain stamp as shown in the workbook.

Discussion Questions

» What whole grains do you like? How often do you eat them?

» What whole grains have you heard about or seen that you'd like to try?

» Which of your products contained whole grains? How do you know?

» Were you surprised by any of the products?

Make Moving Fun!

All Ages

Read a handout on the importance of daily exercise, and then discuss favorite ways to get movement in each day.

Materials

» workbook p. 62

Desired Outcomes

» Participants identify physical activity as an essential component of a healthy life.

» Participants identify different ways they can increase the amount of physical activity in their lives.

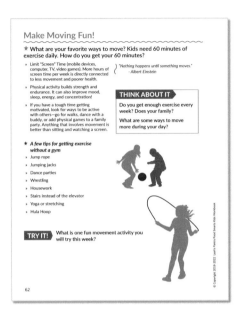

Directions

1. Facilitate a discussion with the following questions:

   » What kinds of movement do you enjoy the most?

   » In what ways do you notice that your activity level affects how you feel during the day?

   » What do you find to be the most challenging about being more physically active?

   » What do you appreciate about moving your body?

2. Read the bullet point on the page. Have participants consider the "Think About It" questions.

3. Ask each to write a smart goal related to movement.

Facilitation Tips

» Encourage participants to examine how exercise might help their mood, energy, feelings of accomplishment, strength, and enjoyment

» Encourage participants to start small if they have a hard time getting started or sustaining physical activity.

» Remind participants to notice and celebrate even small joys and successes around being active and to build upon them a little at a time.

Make These Meals Healthier

Review sample meals and suggest ways of making them healthier

◼ Materials

» workbook p. 29, optional pages 12-13, 26

» paper and pencils

◼ Desired Outcomes

» Participants identify ways to increase whole foods and food variety by making substitutions.

◼ Directions

» Individually or in small groups, participants can improve the meals listed on the workbook page. Have them refer to the Leah's Pantry Do Eat Food List pages 12-13 or MyPlate p. 26 for ideas.

◼ Facilitation Tips

» Encourage participants to revise the meals based on their preferences, habits, and budget.

» Explain that there is no one perfect meal. Making small changes in a meal can help improve our diets over time.

Adapting for Younger Kids

» Read aloud one of the meal examples and have kids draw it.

» Ask them to look at the meal and figure out which MyPlate food groups are represented. Which are missing?

» Then have kids identify which rainbow colors of fruits and vegetables are represented. Which are missing?

» Have kids work with partners or groups to improve the meal by drawing in more food groups and/or colorful fruits and vegetables.

Measuring

Practice using measuring spoons and cups.

Materials

» measuring cups and spoons

» liquid and dry ingredients

Desired Outcomes

» Participants can accurately measure liquid and dry ingredients.

Directions

» For this exercise, participants learn the basics of using measuring cups and spoons. With a small class, you can lead the demonstration and ask participants to participate as you go along. In the event of a large class, you can separate the class into stations with a set of measuring cups and spoons for each.

Liquid Measurements

» Using water or other ingredients from the recipe of this session, demonstrate the proper way to measure liquid ingredients.

1. Fill the liquid measuring cup up to the line.

2. Place it on a level surface.

3. Bend do so you are at eye level with the measurement to read it accurately.

Dry Measurements

» Using flour, grains, sugar, brown sugar and/or other ingredients from this session's recipe, demonstrate measuring with a set of measuring cups and measuring spoons.

1. Scoop the ingredient with the measuring cup or spoon. Or for a large measuring cup, spoon it in.

2. Use the flat back of a utensil to sweep the excess off the top.

Measuring Game

» After reviewing liquid and dry measurements with the whole class, put them up to the challenge and select participants at random to demonstrate measuring amounts of various ingredients for the class. Vary the ingredients and amounts with each student, and see how everyone measures up!

My Family's Rainbow/Eat the Rainbow!

Categorize fruits and vegetables according to color and the nutrients they provide and determine which colors might be missing from the diet.

▌ Materials

» workbook p. 35-36

▌ Desired Outcomes

» Participants learn to associate eating a variety of colorful fruits and vegetables with obtaining a variety of nutrients.

» Participants identify whether they're getting all their vitamins by determining if they "eat the rainbow."

▌ Directions

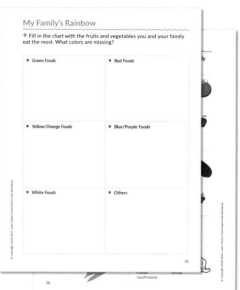

1. Have participants fill in the chart with examples of their family's favorites. Which colors are missing?

   » Orange and yellow foods contain carotenoids (including beta-carotene) which gives them their color and is converted to vitamin A in the body, where it helps keep our eyes and blood healthy. Eggs, spinach, and milk also contain this vitamin.

   » Green foods have:

      » Vitamin B: helps release food's energy so our body can use it. It also helps our body make red blood cells, which is crucial to making sure oxygen is carried throughout our bodies. (Whole grains, fish, meat, eggs, citrus fruits and dairy products also contain Vitamin B.)

      » Vitamin E: maintains our body's tissues in our eyes, skin, and liver. It also protects our lungs from air pollution. (Whole grains, egg yolks and nuts also contain this vitamin.)

      » Vitamin K: helps our blood clot when we get a cut! (Liver, pork, and dairy products also contain this vitamin.)

   » Red and orange citrus fruits often contain Vitamin C, which keeps our body's tissues (like our muscles and gums) in good shape. It also works hard to keep our immune system strong and heal us when we get hurt. (Broccoli and cabbage also contain Vitamin C.)

   » Blue and purple fruits and vegetables are rich in phytonutrients and other compounds which have been studied extensively for their anti-cancer properties, repairing cell damage, preventing blood clots and lowering blood pressure.

   » White foods often get a bad rap but they can be high in Vitamin C and Potassium, and important mineral for heart and muscle function. They also contain anti inflammatory and cancer fighting compounds.

2. Explain the following.

   » Some vitamins are stored in the fat tissues of your body and wait until your body needs them (A, D, E, K).

   » Other vitamins (B, C) travel through your bloodstream and are either used immediately or discarded by your body. Make sure to eat these vitamins every day!

   » What kinds of foods do we need to make sure we eat every day to have enough vitamins that we need? Whole grains; leafy greens; citrus fruits; or other fruits containing Vitamin C.

MyPlate/Healthy Eating Plate

Ages 9+

Participants compare and discuss differences between MyPlate and Healthy Eating Plate using a handout on each.

Materials

» workbook p. 26-27

» chart comparing MyPlate and Healthy Eating Plate (below and available at: https://www.hsph.harvard.edu/nutritionsource/healthy-eating-plate-vs-usda-MyPlate/)

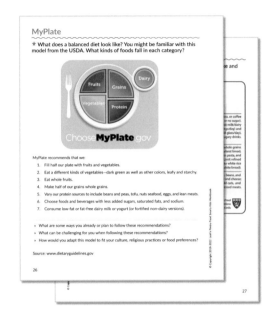

Desired Outcomes

» Participants compare MyPlate and Healthy Eating Plate.

» Participants deepen their understanding of food groups.

Directions

» Have participants compare the two models. You may use the chart below to prompt discussion.

Healthy Eating Plate	MyPlate
Whole Grains The Healthy Eating Plate encourages consumers to choose whole grains and limit refined grains, since whole grains are much better for health. In the body, refined grains like white bread and white rice act just like sugar. Over time, eating too much of these refined-grain foods can make it harder to control weight and can raise the risk of heart disease and diabetes.	**Grains** MyPlate does not tell consumers specifically that whole grains are better for health.
Fruits The Healthy Eating Plate recommends eating a colorful variety of fruits.	**Fruits** MyPlate also recommends eating fruits.
Healthy Protein The Healthy Eating Plate encourages consumers to choose fish, poultry, beans or nuts, and other sources of healthy protein. It encourages them to limit red meat and avoid processed meat, since eating even small quantities of these foods on a regular basis raises the risk of heart disease, diabetes, colon cancer, and weight gain.	**Protein** MyPlate's protein section could be filled by a hamburger or hot dog; it offers no indication that some high-protein foods are healthier than others, or that red and processed meat are especially harmful to health.
Vegetables The Healthy Eating Plate encourages an abundant variety of vegetables, since Americans are particularly deficient in their vegetable consumption—except for potatoes and French fries. Potatoes are chock full of rapidly digested starch, and they have the same effect on blood sugar as refined grains and sweets, so limited consumption is recommended.	**Vegetables** MyPlate does not distinguish between potatoes and other vegetables.

Healthy Eating Plate	MyPlate
Healthy Oils	**(Not Included on MyPlate)**
The Healthy Eating Plate depicts a bottle of healthy oil, and it encourages consumers to use olive, canola, and other plant oils in cooking, on salads, and at the table. These healthy fats reduce harmful cholesterol and are good for the heart, and Americans don't consume enough of them each day. It also recommends limiting butter and avoiding trans fat.	MyPlate is silent on fat, which could steer consumers toward the type of low-fat, high carbohydrate diet that makes it harder to control weight and worsens blood cholesterol profiles.
Water	**Dairy**
The Healthy Eating Plate encourages consumers to drink water, since it's naturally calorie free, or to try coffee and tea (with little or no sugar), which are also great calorie-free alternatives. (Questions about caffeine and kids? Read more.) It advises consumers to avoid sugary drinks, since these are major contributors to the obesity and diabetes epidemics. It recommends limiting milk and dairy to one to two servings per day, since high intakes are associated with increased risk of prostate cancer and possibly ovarian cancer; it recommends limiting juice, even 100% fruit juice, to just a small glass a day, because juice contains as much sugar and as many calories as sugary soda.	MyPlate recommends dairy at every meal, even though there is little if any evidence that high dairy intakes protect against osteoporosis, and there is considerable evidence that too high intakes can be harmful. MyPlate says nothing about sugary drinks or juice.
Stay Active	**(Not included on MyPlate)**
The figure scampering across the bottom of the Healthy Eating Plate's placemat is a reminder that staying active is half of the secret to weight control. The other half is eating a healthy diet with modest portions that meet your calorie needs.	There is no activity message on MyPlate.

Share these key takeaways

- » Both MyPlate and Healthy Eating Plate recommend filling half the plate with fruits and vegetables.

- » Both recommend eating some grains and high-protein foods.

- » Even though both images show all the food groups, it is not necessary for every meal to include every food group. Rather, go for overall balance through the day.

Discussion Questions

- » What are some ways you already or plan to follow the MyPlate or Healthy Eating Plate recommendations?

- » What can be challenging for you when following these recommendations?

- » What are meals that you eat that fit these models?

- » What are examples of meals that may not fit these models but still contain a healthful variety (i.e. traditional dishes, one bowl meals, stews)?

Nutrition Words to Know

Learn about some of the nutrition terms found on a label by matching them with their definitions.

▌ Materials

» workbook p. 51

» several examples of food packages

▌ Desired Outcomes

» Participants define words found on labels of food packages.

▌ Directions

1. Pass out the food packaging samples. Having kids work with partners or in small groups, have them write down any words they can find on the packaging that they are not sure the meaning of. Remind them that just because they recognize a word, they may still not know the meaning— this will definitely be true for words they see on the Nutrition Facts and ingredients lists!

2. Then review the workbook page as a whole group, asking participants to take turns matching the words to the definitions.

▌ Discussion Questions

» Did you learn anything new about the nutrition words? Which ones?

» Were there any words on your list from the packaging activity that were not explained on the workbook page?

» How could you learn more about the additional words you listed?

Plant Parts We Eat

All Ages

Guess which part of a plant different fruits and vegetables come from.

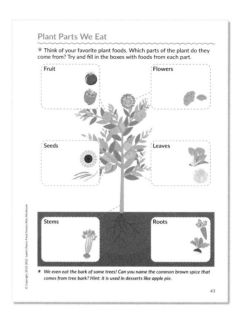

Materials

» workbook p. 43

» pictures or examples of different fruits and vegetables

Desired Outcomes

» Participants learn about different plant parts of the plant that we eat.

Directions

1. Working alone or with partners, have kids complete the workbook page. You may wish to prompt them by providing a few more examples for each part, such as:

   » **Roots and bulbs:** onion, yam, carrot, radish, ginger, garlic, beet, potato

   » **Leaves:** all green leafy vegetables such as spinach, cabbage, kale, lettuce; herbs such as mint, basil

   » **Fruits:** peppers, tomato, squash, cucumber, apple, peach, etc.

   » **Stems and stalks:** celery, asparagus, some herbs (like cilantro stems)

   » **Seeds:** corn, peas, beans, sunflower seeds, pumpkin seeds, sesame seeds, peanuts; some fruits/vegetables with edible seeds such as strawberries and cucumbers; some "seed grains" such as quinoa

   » **Flowers:** broccoli, cauliflower

2. Also help them identify the common spice we use that comes from tree bark: cinnamon.

3. Ask: What is the difference between a fruit and a vegetable? Explain that even though we usually classify foods as fruits and vegetables whether they are sweet or savory, fruits are technically any part of a plant that contain its seeds. This is why tomatoes and cucumbers are classified as vegetables, even though they are actually fruits of the plants they are grown on. Botanists classify foods according to the part of the plant they are.

Discussion Questions

» Which plant parts do you think you eat the most?

» What plants have more than one part you can eat? (examples: fruits and vegetables with edible seeds, carrots and carrot tops, celery, and celery root)

Restaurateur

Invent a menu featuring creative uses of whole foods.

Materials

» paper and pens (big or small paper)

Desired Outcomes

» Participants use creativity and imagination to design balanced meals

Directions

1. With a partner, have participants imagine they were a chef of their own restaurant. Have them identify some concepts about healthy eating that are taught in food smarts to create three meals to put on the menu of their imaginary restaurant. Workbook pages for ideas: Eat the Rainbow, Beans and Grains, Superstar Ingredients, MyPlate, Healthy Eating Plate.

2. Encourage them to be as creative as possible and seek inspiration from favorite cuisines and cultural traditions.

3. Have them draw a picture of how they would present the dish to the diners of their restaurant.

4. Share the meals! Should any of them be made in class next week?

5. Use EatFresh.org to get suggestions for recipes.

Facilitation Tips

» Encourage participants to be creative.

» Suggest they draw pictures of their meal creations.

Rethink Your Drink 🌿

All Ages

Guess the amount of sugar in various drinks and learn how to drink more water.

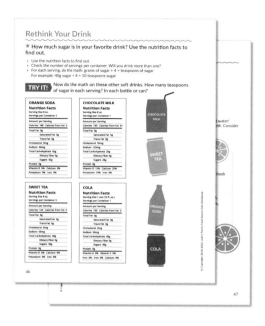

Materials

» workbook p. 46-47

» granulated sugar or sugar cubes

» clear plastic cups

» teaspoon (if using granulated sugar)

Desired Outcomes

» Participants determine and visually represent how much sugar is in a drink.

» Participants identify ways to increase water consumption and reduce sugary beverage consumption

Directions

1. Show the participants one teaspoon of sugar or one sugar cube.

2. Ask the participants how many teaspoons they think are in one can of soda.

3. Write their guesses on the board.

4. Work together to calculate the teaspoons in each soft drink shown.

5. If using sugar cubes, stack the sugar cubes for each drink shown.

6. Optional: Calculate how much sugar someone would consume in a year if they had one of those beverages everyday for a month. There are approximately 109 teaspoons of sugar in a pound.

7. Discuss participants' response to the graphic visualization of how much sugar is in a drink. Ask if this changes their perspective on consuming these drinks.

8. Review page 47 to discuss ways to drink more water to quench thirst. Have participants share ways they increase their water consumption or reduce consumption of sweetened drinks. Add these suggestions:

   » Treat your favorite sweetened beverage as a treat

   » Quench your thirst with water before drinking a favorite sugary beverage

   » Add sparkling or plain water to juices or drinks to cut the sugar

Discussion Questions

» Do you think you drink enough water? Why or why not?

» Is drinking water safety a concern in your area? How do you handle it?

» Do you notice a difference in how you feel when you are thirsty vs. hydrated? Does it help your mood or energy?

» Do you notice a difference in how you feel when you drink sugary drinks?

Rethink Your Drink (CONTINUED)

Adapting for Younger Kids

» Display several examples of soft drinks, including "juice drink," chocolate milk, or sweetened tea if possible, with sugar content for each container pre-measured for kids to see. Alternately, label each with the total teaspoons of sugar and have kids help you count out the total teaspoons of granulated sugar as you measure.

» As an extension, provide each child with a cup containing a few orange slices (skin on). Have kids squeeze the slices into their cups to see how much juice is contained. How many slices/whole oranges do they think it would take to fill up the whole cup with juice? If possible, calculate it out! (An 8 oz. cup requires 3-6 whole oranges.) Help them see that it takes a lot of fruit to make juice—way more than one person would usually sit and eat.

AYK

Seed to Plant to Table

All Ages

Explore where different foods come from.

Materials

» a variety of foods that started as seeds

» a variety of processed/packaged food that did not start as seeds

  » try combinations such as fresh or dried cherries, gummy cherry candies, and cherry-flavored drink

Desired Outcome

» Participants consider the origins of different foods and their paths to our table.

» Participants learn that food from seeds or soil have more nutrition than industrially processed foods.

Directions

1. Ask: Can anyone can think of foods that come from seeds? Of these foods, which ones do you like to eat.

2. Show the class a variety of foods. Ask participants to identify which of the foods started as seeds, and which foods did not.

3. Ask: which foods are good for your body? Why?

   » Foods that grow from seeds or in nature have nutrients from the soil and the sun that give you good energy and prevent us from getting sick. Foods that came from a factory or lab do not have as many.

   » The fewer steps a food takes to get from its beginnings to our table, the more nutrition it provides.

4. Next, discuss the following:

   » Where did this food come from? Did it come from a nearby farm? Was it produced in a factory?

   » Did it come from your state? Somewhere else in this country? Somewhere else in the world?

   » Who helped make this food? Who played a part in getting this food to where it is now (your plate)? Farmers? Truck drivers? Other workers? Consider everyone involved in the production of this food.

   » When you are finished eating this food, what is left over? Do you have a seed to plant to grow this food again?

Sleep Your Way to Health

A crossword puzzle about the importance of sleep.

▮ Materials

» workbook p. 65

» pens

▮ Desired Outcomes

» Participants learn the benefits of getting adequate sleep.

▮ Directions

» Have participants fill in the crossword puzzle individually, in pairs, or as a whole group.

▮ Discussion Questions

» Do you get enough sleep? Why or why not?

» What happens to your body when you don't get enough sleep?

» Which of the following sleep improvement habits could work for you?

  » Turning off screens one hour before bed.

  » Relaxing, reading, meditation, or breathing exercises.

  » Avoiding sugar or caffeine late in the day.

  » Getting exercise (but not before bed).

  » Getting out in the sun during the day.

  » Sleeping in a cool room.

  » Taking a bath.

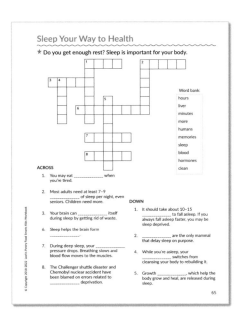

Spice Is Nice

All Ages

A hands on exploration of spices and seasonings that are used in different cultures.

▌ Materials

» several herb and spice samples in small lidded jars (baggies also work but can get messy/smelly; ideally samples are unmarked)

▌ Desired Outcomes

» Participants explore culturally diverse ways of seasoning food and decreasing added salt.

▌ Directions

1. Pass around spice samples for participants to observe and smell. If spices are unmarked, have them guess what's what!

2. Invite them to share their experiences using these and other spices.

3. Point out that many herbs and spices have been used in traditional cuisines and medicines for health-promoting properties. Some scientific research shows that they have health promoting properties—ginger and mint are great for digestion, for example. All can be used to add flavor instead of adding more salt.

4. Also note that herbs and spices lose their flavor with time and exposure to air; some can be added at the beginning of a recipe, while others are saved for the end to preserve the flavors.

▌ Discussion Questions

» What spices did your family use growing up?

» What spices do you associate with Mexican cuisine? South Asian or Indian cuisine? Chinese cuisine?

» What spices can be used in desserts to add flavor (and decrease the need for sugar)?

» Which spices would you like to experiment with?

» What other ingredients can you add to food to make flavor "pop"? (Examples: lemon juice, vinegar, a pinch of sweetener.)

Taste Test

Sample new foods through the 5 senses.

Materials

» workbook p. 7

» simple whole foods, cut or portioned into bite sizes

Use seasonal foods when possible, such as:

» **Spring:** greens: spinach, chard, dandelion, different varieties of lettuce, asparagus

» **Summer:** berries: strawberries, raspberries, blackberries, blueberries, gooseberries, tomatoes; corn, cherries

» **Fall:** pumpkin, squashes, apples, pears, grapes

» **Winter:** citrus fruits: clementines, mandarins, satsumas, persimmons: fuyu and ripe hachiya; pomegranates

» **Year-round:** milks: skim, low-fat, whole, soy, rice, and almond beverages; nuts: raw almonds, cashews; yogurt, cooked whole grains, whole grain crackers or bread

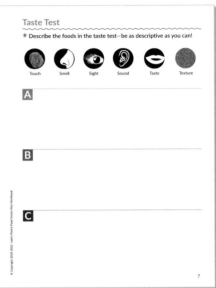

Desired Outcomes

» Participants experience whole food through all 5 senses.

» Participants try new foods.

Directions

1. At the beginning of class, provide bite-sized sample portions of your taste test item.

2. Ask participants to eat slowly and not comment on the food immediately, but rather observe it using their senses. Ask them to write notes in the workbook:

   » **Touch:** What is the temperature like? Is the food soft or hard? Wet or dry?

   » **Smell:** What does it smell like? Does it remind you of anything?

   » **Sight:** What color is the food? What makes it look appealing or not appealing? Can you tell what it is?

   » **Sound:** Does it make a sound when you eat it?

   » **Taste:** Does it remind you of any other foods? How would you describe the taste? Does the taste change as it's in your mouth?

   » **Texture:** How does it feel in your mouth? Smooth? hard? crumbly? crunchy?

3. Once everyone has had a chance to try the item, invite participants to share their observations.

All Ages

Facilitation Tips

» Encourage interaction and fun exploration. This activity is meant to expose participants to the pleasure of eating new things and seasonal fruits and vegetables.

» You may find it helpful to coordinate the taste tests with the recipe for each week; for example, if you are making hummus & veggie wraps for a class at the end of summer, you might provide a taste test of different kinds of tomatoes—different colors, heirloom varieties, etc.—and you can then use those same kinds of tomatoes for the recipe, bringing the class full circle.

EatFresh.org Recipe & Taste Test Combination Suggestions

Berries, Fruits	Fruit and Yogurt Parfaits
Tomatoes	Hummus & Veggie Wraps; Tabbouleh
Vegetables	Pita Pizzas
Persimmons	Spinach & Persimmon Salad
Apples	Curried Waldorf Salad; Spicy Sweet Potato & Apple Soup
Avocados	Avocado & Orange Soup
Beans, Vegetables	Black Bean Soup
Tomatoes, Mangoes	Salsa Two Ways
Fruits, Grains	Oat Bran Banana Muffins
Berries, Tofu, Soy Milks	Tofu Berry Smoothie

Thinking About Being Active

Interactive group activity exploring the challenges and benefits of being active.

Materials

» paper, one per group (large pieces ideal, but anything will work)

» markers

Desired Outcomes

» Participants recognize the challenges of being active and brainstorm solutions.

Directions

1. Divide the class into four groups.

2. Hand out manila paper and markers to each group. (If the class is less than eight people, have two groups answer two questions each.)

3. Assign one of the lists below to each group and have them brainstorm answers:

    » Things that Make It Easy to be Active

    » Things that Make It Hard to be Active

    » Why Being Active Every Day Is Important

    » Easy Ways to Be Active Every Day

Discussion Questions

» What is a tip that you might give to someone struggling with being more physically active? Offer these tips afterwards:

    » Getting into a routine is the first step. Start small with an easy activity and try to do it daily or at minimum, every other day.

    » When you do something physically active, tell another person about it.

Weight and Body Size

A positive and realistic discussion about body size, weight, and weight loss.

Materials

» workbook p. 14

Desired Outcomes

» Participants learn that health is more than weight and size.

» Participants expand their understanding of ways to care for their body including a sustainable approach to weight management

Directions

1. Have participants review the page silently or as a group.

2. Ask participants to identify one idea from the page that is meaningful to them or something that they might not have thought about before.

3. If this topic is particularly sensitive for participants, consider allowing them to ask questions or make comments anonymously on pieces of paper.

Discussion Questions

» How have you seen weight loss portrayed in the media? What is realistic about these portrayals? What might not be realistic?

» What are some beliefs and stereotypes about different body shapes and sizes that you have heard?

» How do these beliefs and stereotypes make you feel? How do they affect how you treat your body?

» What are things you appreciate about your body? How could you honor and nurture these things?

Facilitation Tips

» Encourage realistic conversation about weight loss with the following messages:

   » Every body responds differently to diet and exercise but the benefits of diet and exercise go far beyond weight management.

   » Weight depends on many underlying factors besides exercise and diet such as sleep, stress, genetics and health conditions.

   » Healthy behaviors such as getting enough sleep, moving your body, and eating nourishing foods go a long way to improving health, energy and mobility. Dramatic weight loss is not a requirement for achieving health.

What's on MyPlate

Read about MyPlate food groups and draw a MyPlate meal.

◼ Materials

» workbook p. 24-25

» optional: pictures of simple foods for kids to sort according to food groups

◼ Desired Outcomes

» Participants learn about the food groups included in MyPlate.

» Participants observe that half of MyPlate consists of fruits and vegetables.

◼ Directions

1. Ask participants to share what they know about "food groups"—some will be very familiar with this concept already, while younger kids may not.

2. Then have participants look at the MyPlate sheet with the groups listed on it. Discuss each of the five groups shown and share some examples. Have participants share examples they think belong to each group as well. If you have pictures to display, ask them to identify which group each item belongs to.

3. Once you feel participants are comfortable with the concepts, ask them to use the blank MyPlate to create a balanced meal, or one that includes ingredients from each group. They can write or draw their ideas.

4. Have volunteers share their finished meals with the group.

◼ Discussion Questions

» What are some foods that are hard to put into one food group? Why?

» Does every meal need to have all five groups? Why or why not?

» A snack should include at least two of the groups so that you can feel full and get energy. What two groups do you like to have together?

» Which group is it easy to get enough of every day? Which group is hard for you to get enough of?

Your Healthy Life/Your Healthy Goals *All Ages*

Envision a healthy life, create SMART goals towards that vision, and track weekly progress.

▌Materials

» workbook p. 9-11

▌Desired Outcomes

» Participants identify their big picture vision of health and translate it into smaller achievable steps (SMART Goals).

» Participants create a SMART goal and track it weekly during the workshop series.

▌Directions

1. Have participants follow directions in workbook page 9 to imagine their healthy life.

2. Using page 10, explain SMART goals and work with the class to find some examples.

3. Help each individual create at least one SMART goal that helps them move towards their vision they will try to achieve during the course of the workshop. Refer to examples or suggest others.

4. Have each participant record their goal using the tracking sheet on page 11. Have them check in each week with a partner using the check-in questions on the Goal Tracker.

▌Discussion Question

» Who around you can you call on to support you around your SMART goals?

▌Facilitation Tips

» Some participants may be very focused on dieting and weight loss. Review the Weight and Body Size on p. 14 in the workbook prior to class to be ready to offer appropriate messages about weight loss.

» Suggest participants flip through the workbook to find some ideas if they get stuck.

» As the workshop progresses, participants may want to change their goal or refine the same one. Encourage them to find something that is do able for their own circumstances.

» Remind participants that the purpose of this activity is to not be perfect at one's goal but to adopt an attitude of growth and flexibility over time.

» For kids, the value of this activity is to be encouraged to try new things and experiment with setting goals for their future wellbeing.

Adapting for Younger Kids

Younger participants may not understand abstract differences between vague goals and specific ones, and they don't have much control over food that is offered to them. Instead, consider setting a group goal that can be accomplished in the context of the class. For example:

» I will drink a cup of water every afternoon with my snack.
» I will try one new food today.

Made in the USA
Columbia, SC
26 October 2024

45106421R00062